TO THE ENDS OF THE EARTH

MEMOIRS OF A PIONEERING AVIATOR

To John

Happy Birthday

Robert

21ˢᵗ March 2020

TO THE ENDS OF THE EARTH

MEMOIRS OF A PIONEERING AVIATOR

SIR ALAN COBHAM

TEMPUS

First published as two separate volumes by A.&C. Black, Ltd 1926
This edition 2007

Tempus Publishing
Cirencester Road, Chalford
Stroud, Gloucestershire, GL6 8PE
www.tempus-publishing.com

Tempus Publishing is an imprint of NPI Media Group

British Library Cataloguing in Publication Data.
A catalogue record for this book is available from the British Library.

ISBN 978 0 7524 4400 0

Typesetting and origination by NPI Media Group
Printed and bound in Great Britain

CONTENTS

I wish to dedicate this little book to Sir Charles Wakefield, Bart., who for many years has done all in his power to further the development of aviation in which he is such an ardent believer.

April 1926.

ALAN J. COBHAM.

MY FLIGHT TO THE CAPE AND BACK

Reproduced by kind permission of Lady Cobham.

Following his pioneering round-trip voyages to India, South Africa and Australia, Alan John Cobham (later Sir Alan) was recognised as Britain's premier airman in the inter-war period.

NOTE

Mr Cobham has written a personal and unvarnished account of his memorable flight to Cape Town and back. This is illustrated almost entirely from photographs taken by members of the expedition.

As a survey of the possibilities of great intermediate air routes throughout Africa, in its commercial significance, and as a contribution to our national and imperial prestige the flight was of the first importance. There is good reason, therefore, that everyone should be enabled to possess the record of this modern Elizabethan adventurer.

*Cobham's journey to the Cape (solid line) and return
16 November 1925–13 March 1926. (Airways)*

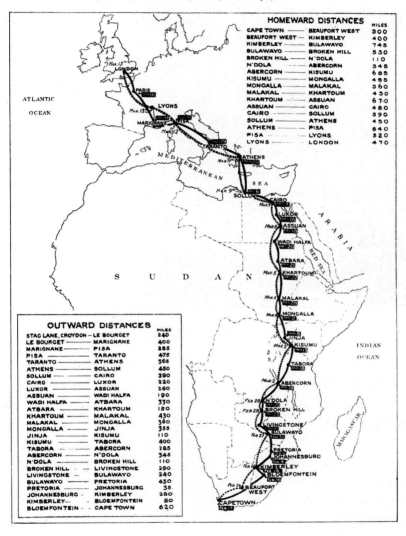

HOMEWARD DISTANCES

		MILES
CAPE TOWN	BEAUFORT WEST	300
BEAUFORT WEST	KIMBERLEY	400
KIMBERLEY	BULAWAYO	745
BULAWAYO	BROKEN HILL	530
BROKEN HILL	N'DOLA	110
N'DOLA	ABERCORN	345
ABERCORN	KISUMU	685
KISUMU	MONGALLA	455
MONGALLA	MALAKAL	360
MALAKAL	KHARTOUM	430
KHARTOUM	ASSUAN	670
ASSUAN	CAIRO	480
CAIRO	SOLLUM	390
SOLLUM	ATHENS	450
ATHENS	PISA	840
PISA	LYONS	320
LYONS	LONDON	470

OUTWARD DISTANCES

		MILES
STAG LANE, CROYDON	LE BOURGET	240
LE BOURGET	MARIGNANE	400
MARIGNANE	PISA	285
PISA	TARANTO	475
TARANTO	ATHENS	365
ATHENS	SOLLUM	450
SOLLUM	CAIRO	390
CAIRO	LUXOR	220
LUXOR	ASSUAN	260
ASSUAN	WADI HALFA	190
WADI HALFA	ATBARA	330
ATBARA	KHARTOUM	150
KHARTOUM	MALAKAL	430
MALAKAL	MONGALLA	360
MONGALLA	JINJA	355
JINJA	KISUMU	110
KISUMU	TABORA	400
TABORA	ABERCORN	285
ABERCORN	N'DOLA	345
N'DOLA	BROKEN HILL	110
BROKEN HILL	LIVINGSTONE	290
LIVINGSTONE	BULAWAYO	240
BULAWAYO	PRETORIA	430
PRETORIA	JOHANNESBURG	35
JOHANNESBURG	KIMBERLEY	280
KIMBERLEY	BLOEMFONTEIN	80
BLOEMFONTEIN	CAPE TOWN	620

DH50 J, G-EBFO, in pristine condition prior to its 16,000-mile journey.

Members of the expedition, from left to right: Alan Cobham; B.W.G. Emmott; A.B. Elliott.

CHAPTER I

LONDON TO CAIRO

A JOURNEY from London through Egypt and the heart of Africa to Cape Town has for centuries appealed to the world as a great adventure. And so a few years ago, when I contemplated this trip with an aeroplane as my means of transport, everyone looked upon the journey as a somewhat hazardous undertaking.

For ages we have heard of 'darkest Africa'. Little seemed to be known of the geography of this part of the world by the general public, and so possibly it was quite natural that my scheme should be regarded as somewhat impracticable, although Sir Pierre Van Ryneveld and Sir Quintin Brand managed to fly to the Cape with great difficulty six years ago.

For over four years I had been contemplating the London–Cape Town flight, and had many times gone into the details of organisation and considered the type of aircraft best suited for the job. My progress was always checked when it came to the question of finance, for it was so difficult to find a really sound reason with which to persuade any company or individual to finance such a scheme, apart from the fact that it was good long-sighted policy and sound propaganda for British aviation.

However, last year I induced twenty-one different companies directly or indirectly connected with aviation to support a flight of survey from London to Cape Town and back. On my struggles in the summer of 1925 in grappling with the difficulties, not only of getting finance, but of putting down supplies through regions of uncharted territory, organising the preparation of old and disused landing grounds, communicating with hosts of officials and various forwarding agencies, I will not dwell, except to say that in a some-what impaired condition of health, owing to the terrific worry and work of this organisation, by 15 November I found myself ready to start.

In the light of my experiences on a recent previous flight from London to Rangoon and back, when I took Air Vice-Marshal Sir Sefton Brancker on a flight of survey, I came to the conclusion that I could select no better craft for this occasion than that which I used on the Rangoon expedition, namely a de Havilland type 50, and we took the identical machine. It was necessary, however, to make an alteration in the power plant. In view of the fact that I should have to take off from high-altitude landing grounds in Central and South Africa, where the density of the atmosphere is so rarefied that in the heat of the day it is equivalent to that at a height of 10,000 feet at home, it was obvious that I should need extra power to get off.

On the Rangoon flight most of the landing grounds, especially those in the hot countries, were in heavy air at sea level the entire way, and we used a 230 H.P. Siddeley Puma engine which did its work very well. But for the Cape flight I decided to have installed a 385 H.P. Siddeley Jaguar, which is an air cooled engine, with the result that my de Havilland would have approximately another 160 H.P. for exactly the same over-all weight.

Before telling the tale of our adventures I must introduce the other two members of the expedition, Mr A.B. Elliott, who was the engineer on the Rangoon flight, and who had been with me on many other occasions, was the engineer on this trip also. It had been decided that a cinematograph film should be made of the whole venture so that the British public might share in a minor degree all our experiences. Thus it came about that the Gaumont Company selected Mr B.W.G. Emmott from their staff to come with us to make the picture.

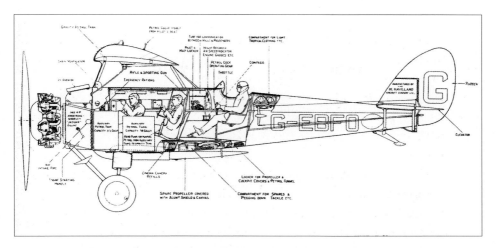

Sectional diagram showing the internal arrangements of the DH50. (*Airways*)

For those who have never seen the de Havilland type 50, let me give a brief outline of the machine. It is a biplane – that is, it has four wings and a body – and the passenger cabin is immediately behind the engine, and between the upper and lower planes. The pilot's cockpit is separate and right behind the cabin, but there is a little communicating window inside the cockpit to the rear of the cabin, so that it was possible for me to converse with my crew during flight. The pilot's seat is high up, so that when the machine was in flight I had an uninterrupted view ahead, over the top of the cabin in front of me.

Our departure from Stag Lane Aerodrome was of great interest and no little amusement to those who saw us off. Stowing the spares, luggage and equipment on board seemed to be the chief business of the day. Firstly we carried underneath the cabin a spare propeller, which had been carefully covered in canvas and screened off. Then there was a certain number of small spare parts that might be required for the machine and engine. Emmott seemed to have a terrific amount of camera gear to pack away, for, apart from the cinematograph camera, there were many thousands of feet of film to be carried and a hefty ungainly tripod. Then there was my own little ciné camera and still camera, Emmott's press camera, and I believe

Cobham at Stag Lane, just prior to leaving for his official departure from Croydon. He appears well prepared for a chilly ride in the DH50's open cockpit.

Gladys Cobham, centre, along with other relatives of pilot Cobham and ciné-photographer A.B. Emmott wave farewell at Stag Lane.

Elliott had one also. Then again we had guns to go on board, because I came to the conclusion that, should we by any misfortune have to land in some uninhabited country or tractless jungle, the guns would not only be a protection but might be our only means of getting food after we had exhausted our few days' emergency rations. Therefore we carried a gun, a rifle and a revolver. There were the emergency cooking utensils, consisting of very light aluminium kettle, pots, mugs and frying pan, besides light aluminium water bottles, and emergency rations in the form of compressed food.

Considerable excitement prevailed when, on that cold grey November morning, three large pith sun helmets were stowed in a special compartment in the back of the machine, with a parcel containing mosquito nets. I think too, that Emmott's and Elliott's light flannel suits and my own khaki drill caused a good deal of comment, but we had heavy underwear and heavy overcoats to keep us warm until we were out of Europe.

Our baggage had been cut down to the finest limits: each had one suit case which when full weighed not more than twenty pounds and measured about twenty inches long by fourteen inches wide and six inches deep. However, there was room for a light alpaca dinner-jacket and evening accessories, so that we could appear more or less respectable when occasion demanded.

We took off from Stag Lane Aerodrome with the intention of flying across London to Croydon to make our official departure, but no sooner had we left the ground and got a few feet in the air than we discovered that London was enveloped in fog and that to reach Croydon it would be necessary to make a detour round the east-end, owing to the fact that an east wind was blowing and smoke and fog completely enveloped the rest of London.

It was not exactly an encouraging start for such a long flight. After flying from Stag Lane in a circular tour for about half an hour on a trip which should have taken only fifteen minutes, I somehow came over Croydon, and only managed to spot the aerodrome by the rockets which they were firing especially for my assistance. After landing, passing Customs and other little formalities we were all ready for the start; in fact I was getting somewhat impatient to get away, for I am never very keen on the 'official goodbye' business. Perhaps my impatience accounted for the fact that I opened my engine a little too quickly as I was taking off on that very cold morning, and consequently momentarily choked her, so that I had to shut off and open out again more slowly. With our reserve of power, however, we were in the air like a rocket and heading for Lympne, only too thankful to be away at last.

On the first day we only reached Paris, and refrained from carrying on to Lyons, because I felt that we were all so tired after the final rush of getting away – though there were others who said we could not resist the temptation of a night in Paris!

On the following day we flew on to Lyons in indifferent weather, and as the hour was too late for us to make Pisa, our intended next stop, we pushed on to Marseilles instead and there spent the night. Bad weather welcomed us next morning, but after it had cleared a little we flew on again for Pisa.

This flight gave me an opportunity to prove what I have said so many times, that the worst bumps in the air are not experienced necessarily in the heat of the tropics, or from hot or cold air rising, but through up and down currents caused by gales dashing over mountains. As a rule the Riviera coastline is one of the great fine weather spots of the world, and the view from an aeroplane flying at a few thousand feet, two or three miles out to sea, is a sight that will never be forgotten by anyone who is fortunate enough to witness it.

As one looks northwards towards the land, there is a deep blue sea in the foreground below such as is not known round the British Isles, and its silver crested breakers dash in a mass of white foam on a rocky shore. From an altitude of 3,000 or 4,000 feet Monte Carlo looks like a collection of fairy palaces clustered on the cliff side, with a little model harbour where perhaps one or two trim steam yachts lie at anchor, and beyond the breakwater, contrasting so vividly with the blue ocean, the snow-white sails of various skiffs.

As one's eye travels beyond the town, there appears a view of massive precipitous cliffs, cut with mountain roadways that are really fine engineering feats. High up on these mountain slopes can be seen ancient little villages, very often built on pinnacles, belonging to a bygone age when the native of this coastline had to take refuge in his own small stronghold from the barbarian who might invade him from Northern Europe or from the pirate and adventurer of the sea. Higher still are fresh mountain ranges with deep valleys, and beyond are the snow-capped Alps whose vividness is intensified by the brilliant sunshine, so that the cloudless blue sky against which these peaks are silhouetted seems to merge into a turquoise hue on the horizon.

When we flew along this coastline one day last November, a vastly different spectacle was to be seen. The sky was overcast and grey, while the Alps were buried in low cloud and mist; but the weather condition which caused us real trouble was the violent, strong north-east wind which for hundreds of miles was dashing over these ice-clad peaks. The result was that by the time the gale had reached the Mediterranean the whole atmosphere seemed to be carried in one mighty chopped-up downrush to the sea.

The further we proceeded along the coastline the more violent became the atmosphere, and so I thought that by flying low under the cliff we might possibly avoid the main disturbance; but here the down current was so violent that it was difficult to keep the machine on an even keel. I then decided to climb to a high altitude in search of a calmer zone so, opening out the engine and pulling back the control lever, we very quickly shot up to 6,000 feet. But the higher we went the worse became the bumps, and the machine at times seemed to be almost uncontrollable.

Emmott and Elliott in the cabin were having a very rough time, for it was with great difficulty that they could keep in their seats. While Elliott strove to keep the baggage in position, Emmott was struggling with his beloved camera which I thought might be broken at any moment, as very often baggage and passengers' heads touched the roof of the cabin as the machine was caught in some violent down current.

All this took place in a very short space of time, and we quickly decided that the only course of action was to get away from the trouble, the mountains; and so we headed for the open sea. This was not sufficient to get rid of all the bumps, and I resorted to an old plan that I had practised so often before; we flew right out to sea, away from the shore and very low over the water which evidently acts as a cushion for the down currents of the wind, and gives a more or less steady, even atmosphere. In this way we continued across the bay before Genoa, skimming over the sea within twenty feet of the water, in fact so low were we flying that when we encountered a fleet of fishing smacks it was necessary to climb a little to clear their masts. It was here we had the little thrill of flashing by these boats as they were tossed in the rough sea, much to the excitement of the fishermen who waved vigorously to us as we flew on our way.

At last Pisa was reached, and as the day was too short for us to reach our next destination before dark, we decided to stay the night, and if possible see the leaning tower before dusk.

On the following day we had a comparatively simple flight over almost the whole length of Italy to our next landing place, Grottaglie near Taranto at the heel of Italy. Here we were most enthusiastically received by the Italian Commandant who greeted us the moment we landed, while in his trail followed one of the mess stewards, carrying a tray of bottles and glasses with all the requirements necessary for any cocktail that one might mention. We had travelled 500 miles or over 800 kilometres, and our host evidently considered that we needed fortifying. He himself mixed for us some wonderful brandy flip cocktails, whose main ingredients were eggs and brandy, and after partaking of them we all had a distinctly good impression of Grottaglie.

On the following day we set out on our trip from the heel of Italy to Athens, our route lying across the southern Adriatic to Corfu, along the Grecian coastline, and through the Gulfs of Patras and Corinth to Athens. On this journey we again experienced the difficulties of flying on the leeward side of the mountains when a gale is blowing, for the same north-east wind that we encountered above the Riviera coast was raging in the narrow passage of the Gulf of Corinth. Again we had to resort to our old tactics of flying low over the sea to take advantage of the evidently steadying effect that the surface of the water has on the atmosphere when the wind is dashing down upon it.

From Athens we had a 480-mile flight over the sea, by way of Crete to Sollum on the African coast, and thence eastwards along the sea shore to Cairo.

Up to this time we had refrained from taking a cinema picture from the aeroplane during flight, owing to the many restrictions and regulations regarding aerial photography in the various countries we had passed over in Europe, but from the moment we arrived in Egypt, right through to the Cape, we were quite free to do whatever we liked in this matter.

Before leaving England we had taken a short experimental flight round Stag Lane Aerodrome, when Emmott had evidently imagined that all the facilities for taking pictures were quite simple and in order. Before taking off from Sollum we arranged that one of our first shots would be of the desert changing suddenly from the barren sandy waste to the rich fertile delta of the Nile, to be followed by a long shot of the Pyramids in the distance, after which we would take close-ups of them, and finally general scenes of Cairo before landing on the RAF aerodrome at Heliopolis.

Here it will be best to explain something of the system of aerial photography, which, generally speaking, is of two kinds: vertical, which is taken from a special camera at the bottom of the aeroplane and gives a plan view of the ground beneath, and oblique, which gives a panoramic view such as can be obtained from any high hill or tower. On this flight we were interested only in oblique photography, both for cinema and still pictures.

It is quite easy to understand that unless the pilot places the aeroplane in the correct position, it is impossible for the photographer to get the picture, and this is still more the case when the photographer has but a very confined space in which to work, with hardly any traverse at all. Such was the position of Mr Emmott and Mr Elliott when working from the little cabin of our machine. It was so arranged that Emmott could take his ciné pictures from one of the front windows of the cabin, thus getting a forward view, and that Elliot should take the still pictures with the ordinary cameras from one of the rear windows.

As we neared Cairo on a certain afternoon in December the day began to warm up and, because we had not cast our winter clothing and had just come from a very cold climate, we all felt the sudden heat, especially those in the cabin. On approaching the Nile Delta I yelled through my little window into the cabin to tell them to get ready to take pictures, and then the fun commenced.

Whether it was that Emmott did not quite understand that it was necessary to wait until the pilot gave him the picture – for the slightest movement of the control lever would take his object out of view – or that neither he nor Elliot were used to working together in such a confined space, or that it was the heat of the day which overpowered them, or yet again that I was at fault for manoeuvring the machine too fast, none of us seemed to know exactly. However, from the onset I could see that something was amiss in the cabin; no one seemed to take picture when I gave the view, but film was being taken when I was not placing the aeroplane for any particular picture. I throttled down the engine and yelled further instructions through the cabin window amid the roar, the only effect that this procedure seemed to have was to darken the countenances of my two passengers, resulting in a further obstinacy to coincide with my manoeuvres for aerial photography.

On nearing the Pyramids I thought that our chance had come for really fine stuff, and after banking the machine and struggling to the best of my ability for two or three minutes to get what I though would be a magnificent view of this ancient Egyptian masterpiece, I yelled to Emmott to 'take'. On looking through the cabin window I discovered that he had evidently given up the idea of photography, and was gazing vacantly at the landscape, while Elliott on the other hand instead of waiting until I had placed the machine in a convenient position for him, was evidently exposing film on a more or less blank desert.

This was my turn to become annoyed, for the day was hot and I was beginning to perspire in my winter attire through the exertions of banking the machine round and round the Pyramids. So I shouted through in my lustiest tones to Elliott to 'wait for it' and to Emmott to 'take, take, take'.

Instead of stimulating Emmott to action and modifying Elliott to patience, the effect of my shouting had the most alarming results in the cabin. Two perspiring faces turned round and scowled darkly at me, then scowled at one another; then above the roar of the engine I again shouted to explain matters, whereupon they shouted, and for a few moments a perfect inferno raged.

It dawned upon me that possibly I might be to blame for not having arranged with my assistants beforehand and impressed upon them some sound system of co-operation for the aerial photography work, apart from the scanty chat that we had on this subject before starting. Giving up the question of aerial photography for that day, I headed across Cairo for Heliopolis and landed on the RAF aerodrome.

When the machine came to a standstill, I quickly divested myself of some of my outward clothing and was about to explain matters to my crew, when I discovered that both of them, looking very hot, limp and exhausted, had no particular desire to talk to me. However, that was shortlived, because the machine had to be put away and the general routine of the day's work gone through and in the quiet of the hotel that evening we rehearsed with cool and collected heads exactly how our photographic work should be done in the future.

We came to the conclusion that only under exceptional circumstances would Emmott taking cinema film and Elliott taking still photographs be able to operate together at the same moment; I was able to convince Emmott that it was useless for him to try to take pictures until I gave him the view, and that it was the control lever of the aeroplane which really traversed the ciné camera, and kept the view in the sights, because an aeroplane is controllable in three dimensions, the slightest movement of the control lever can make the nose fall or rise, and the wings go up or down, while the rudder can swing the machine to the right or left.

Having ascertained from practical tests with Emmott exactly which view I should have to get from the cockpit at the rear of the machine to coincide with the view that he would get from the front window of the cabin, all was O.K.; I already knew which view I must have to coincide with Elliott's back view from the cabin. Two days later we started off on a short flight over Cairo to film the Pyramids properly, and on this occasion our system worked perfectly. Having decided who should take the first picture, I yelled through to the cabin, 'Emmott, prepare to take', whereupon he would turn the handle as soon as the object came into view, and I would do my utmost to keep the object within his camera sights, at the same time placing the machine so that sun would throw up the best shadows. Then Elliott

The pyramids at Giza.

would be warned and the machine would be placed for his particular view; in this way the procedure was carried out systematically until the subject had been covered by both ciné and still camera.

We discovered a novel method of filming the Pyramids, keeping them in the picture by a system of side-slipping on to them. Owing to the fact that Emmott was taking his film from the front windows of the cabin, we shall be able to give the public a fine view of the Pyramids looking like tiny piles of masonry from thousands of feet above, then through side-slipping down on to them they gradually get larger and larger until at last they fill the picture – the moment when we had to turn away or side-slip into them.

At Heliopolis Aerodrome we were given a wonderful reception by members of the Royal Air Force, who did their very utmost to facilitate our flight to the Cape; my eternal thanks will always be to those officers and men who helped so greatly in the distribution and shipment of my supplies, and to those at H.Q. who had worked up for me so much valuable data regarding the flight ahead.

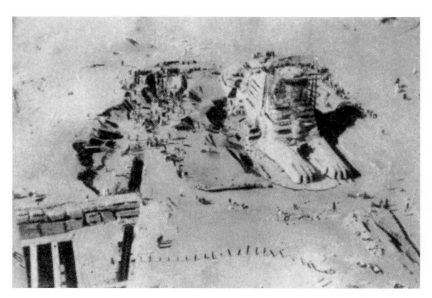

Restoration of the Sphinx.

CHAPTER II

CAIRO TO CAPE TOWN

AFTER nearly a week in Cairo we took off and flew on down the Nile, over the land of the Ancients for Luxor; for Emmott was keen not only to get aerial views of Thebes, Karnak, the Temples of Luxor, the Valley of the Kings, and the Ramasseum, but also to get ground pictures of the relics of the Ancient Egyptian civilization.

Then came a short flight from Luxor to Assuan, where we had the opportunity of filming from the air that masterpiece of British engineering, the Assuan Dam, which stores and controls the water of the irrigation scheme for the whole of Egypt. After this we flew on down the Nile, which from Assuan to Wadi Haifa is turned into one great reservoir, and after spending the night with the Governor at Wadi Haifa we passed on over the Nubian Desert; with ideal weather conditions and perfectly calm atmosphere, we followed the railway across the desert until its meeting with the Nile again at Abu Hamed, and a little further on we landed at Atbara. Atbara is the headquarters of the Sudan Government Railways, and it was here we landed on what is possibly the largest natural aerodrome I have ever seen. It consists of flat, hard, natural desert that seems to extend for miles in every direction.

In these few pages it would be impossible to tell our experiences on every portion of the flight, so I will hurry on to some of my most striking impressions of the journey.

Just before arriving at Khartoum we had the somewhat impressive picture of the meeting of the Blue and White Niles, and here it

Left: In the Ramasseum.

Below: Karnak from the air with the Nile visible in the background.

The Nile at Assuan.

is worth noting that from this point the wonderful river flows about 1,500 miles through the heat of the desert without a single tributary to augment its waters except the River Atbara, which only does so at flood time.

We spent our Christmas at Khartoum, and before the old year had departed we flew on our way southwards to the next landing ground at Malakal. Daily I became more impressed with the enormous opportunities of a great commercial airway that would link up Central Africa with the Mediterranean. Here was a country where it would be possible to maintain a 100 per cent efficiency regularity, and at the same time do a trip in two days that by the present modes of transport takes over three weeks.

At Malakal we landed beside the river on a strip of ground that had been specially prepared but a few weeks before. On the borders of the landing ground was a village of the Shulluks, the natives of this part of the Sudan. In order to give our machine as much protection as possible from any gales that might occur, we drew it close up to their huts; curiously, they showed no interest whatsoever in our aeroplane, and I was told they looked upon it as 'one of the mad things the white men do'.

One of the officials told me that an improvement at which these natives really marvel is the installation of water in pipes. For centuries their womenfolk have journeyed night and morning from the village to the river bank to fetch water, and when water pipes were first laid it was a common thing to see natives gathered round the tap, while one, a little more courageous than the rest, would turn the tap and let the water gush out; this to them was truly marvellous. Water was something that they understood and was the main part of their daily existence, so when it could be obtained merely by the turning of a tap, that indeed was something wonderful. As for an aeroplane, as far as they were concerned it was simply some madness

Shulluks at Malakal.

that was not worth considering, or perhaps it was entirely beyond their comprehension.

On my return journey I landed at Malakal, and the Chief of all the Shulluk tribes happened to be present. He was quite interested in the aeroplane, but I found it impossible to explain to him the distance in mileage that we had come from the Cape in a matter of six days. My interpreter told me to measure it approximately in days of walking, and so, working on the basis of walking continuously about 20 miles a day, I reckoned it would take roughly a year. The interpreter explained to the Chief that we had come a year's march in six days, and I shall never forget the expression on the poor old boy's face as he put his hand to his forehead and shook his head – it was far too much for him.

On the third afternoon after our arrival at Malakal we went down to the landing ground to witness a Shulluk war dance, and as we neared the village we could hear the tom-toms beating to call the braves to the dance. At the village there was a scene of contrasts, for there in the background was one of the white man's latest inventions, an aeroplane, while in the foreground was assembled a tribe of primitive men, preparing to display their greatest pride in life, their prowess as warriors.

The tom-tom continued to beat, and very soon scores of men were marching in a circle round the drummers. Their enthusiasm increased as the dance progressed, and from a mere walk it gradually grew to a manoeuvre far more fantastic and violent. Their dress was majestic in its simplicity, made up of a leopard skin tied round the loins, and a small cloth over the left shoulder. Each man was armed with a spear and carried a shield, but most startling of all was his head-dress. Very often this consisted of a man's own hair plaited with clay and forming shapes as big as a lady's picture hat, or it might be that each little individual ringlet had been taken and interwoven with some kind of wax, so that the head was a mass of short tapers that almost rattled as its owner danced. Some had covered their bodies with ashes, while others had smeared their faces with red brick dust, but notwithstanding their grotesque ideas of decoration they were as a whole a bunch of handsome men.

Presently the circular dance stopped and all the braves retired to the far corner of the open space within the village, while we stood at the opposite end with the aeroplane immediately behind us. Emmott was in his seventh heaven and despite the weight of his heavy camera and ungainly tripod he jumped about from position to position taking different aspects of the dance. When all the braves had assembled at the far end, the beat of the tom-toms changed and the Shulluk warriors advanced a few paces *en masse*, halted and started to chant the war song, gesticulating and shaking their spears. At a given signal from their leader they leaped forward a few more paces and sang more wildly than ever, stamping hard so that the dust rose in clouds around them. A third time they advanced with a mighty shout, each brave trying to outdo his comrade in a spectacular display of prowess with his spear. One could not but admire their wonderful physique, and the play of their superb muscles as several stepped forward individually and gave singular exhibitions, lunging, feinting, side-stepping and finally thrusting forward with their spears. At last, with a frightful roar which made one feel that they were out of control, the whole body of these excited warriors rushed towards us as we stood in front of the aeroplane. Had not the Commissioner been with us I should have had doubts of our safety. It was only his presence that gave me confidence and the assurance that the whole display was but a game, for when it seemed impossible that they could pull up before their spears had buried themselves either in our bodies or in the wings of the aeroplane, they came to a halt with a mighty stamp, their spear points quivering within a few inches of our faces

It took all our nerve to stand perfectly calm before such a spectacle, and the only person who seemed to be unperturbed was Emmott, who had his eye glued to the sight of his cinematograph camera and evidently did not realise how close they were. After this we had the Lion dance and several other performances, and by this time the beat of the tom-tom had brought in from the surrounding villages all the braves who had hastily put on their war dress and come along for the fray. According to custom, I purchased for them a bull upon which they feasted that night in return for the entertainment they had given us.

Our next trip was to Mongalla, and the route lay right over the great Sud area, which is a vast swamp in the Southern Sudan through which the Nile somehow finds its way. Little was known of the route that we should take, and I had heard many tales of the desolate nature of the country over which we should have to pass; but, by keeping well eastward of the Nile, I found that the main portions of the great swamps could be avoided. When we were within a few miles of Mongalla, Elliott spotted a herd of waterbuck on the far side of the Nile and, thinking it would make a good picture for Emmott, I flew over in their direction and came down low in an endeavour to get a close-up picture. The country at this point was open and free from trees, and we were able to fly within twenty feet of the ground and chase the herd. We quickly overtook them, for we could not fly at much less than fifty or sixty miles an hour, and then turned about and chased them the other way, Emmott turning the handle of his machine all the while in the hope of getting a really fine picture of the herd fleeing in absolute terror from the new-come noisy monster of the air.

At Mongalla we realised that our aeroplane was getting decidedly dirty and in need of a wash, so a party of Mongalla beauties was engaged for the work. Afterwards I came to the conclusion that in view of the time it took us to instruct these dusky maidens it would have been far quicker and almost less fatiguing to have done the job ourselves.

The heat was terrific, and at times the wind seemed like tongues of flame fanning one's face, until one longed for sundown when it started to cool a little. The extraordinary thing was that the aeroplane stood up to this gruelling treatment, despite the fact that it was impossible to touch it without burning one's fingers, and when we took off at last from Mongalla, its performance seemed in no way to have depreciated owing to its exposure to the sun.

Mongalla washerwomen.

Mongalla was the last of our low-altitude aerodromes, for it was 1,000 feet above sea level, whereas our next stopping place, Jinja, a few miles north of the equator on the shores of the Victoria Nyanza, was over 4,000 feet above sea level.

This quick change in the altitude of the landing grounds was almost instrumental in causing an accident. It came about in this way. Thousands of natives had assembled from all parts of Uganda to witness our arrival, and the sides of our runways were lined deep with native folk attired in their gaily-coloured costumes. Just as I was coming in low over a banana grove, which bordered the landing ground, several natives rushed across my fairway at the last moment. Thinking that I should most certainly run in to them, I did what I should have done at home or in Europe and landed a little bit shorter, with the object of pulling up before I reached them. Landing shorter meant landing slower, and in the sudden moment of emergency I forgot that I was well over 4,000 feet above sea level in a rarefied atmosphere with a consequently much higher flying speed necessary to keep me in the air.

The result was that when I pulled out of my little side-slip my machine literally fell out of the air for the last ten feet, and it was only the robustness of the undercarriage that saved the situation. After this I determined that while using these high-altitude aerodromes I would land fast, whether natives ran across my fairway or not.

Jinja is beautifully situated amid charming scenery on the shores of the great lake, and I shall always have a vision of the country beneath us as we neared the Victoria Nyanza on our flight from Mongalla. We had come over some of the swamp lakes of Central Uganda and ultimately followed up the course of the Victoria Nile, passing over one beautiful rapid after another until at last the lake came into view, seeming to spill its waters over the famous Ripon Falls, where in reality is the source of the Great Nile.

From Jinja we flew on round the lake to Kisumu, which is about five miles south of the equator. Kisumu is the main port on the Victoria Nyanza lake, and boasts of having the highest dry dock in the world.

We were always being surprised by the startling lack of knowledge of even the simplest rudiments of flying displayed by the various people that we met en route, and many are the stories that we could tell in connection with this topic. The remark of one dear lady at Kisumu is well worth mentioning. After asking me a few perfectly obvious questions about flying, she then said, 'How do you manage to sleep at night?' I replied, 'Oh, we always manage to get put up by the local authorities, either staying in a rest house or enjoying the hospitality of somebody's private residence.' The good lady looked bewildered for a moment, and then, with a somewhat disappointed expression on her face, remarked, 'Oh, so you *come down* at night then.'

Kisumu was virtually the end of our survey of the great air line of the future that will run from Cairo to the Victoria Nyanza, thus bringing the whole of Central Africa within about seven days of England, instead of a month as at present. After my flight over this route I felt that it would be a sound and practical proposition, not only from an aviation point of view but also commercially, to open up one of the finest air transport routes of the age.

From Kisumu we flew to Tabora in the heart of Tanganyika, and here we entered the dense forest areas that stretch for hundreds of miles in all directions right down into Rhodesia. Beyond Tabora the country for two hundred miles or more has been depopulated purposely, in an endeavour to stamp out sleepy sickness by preventing the fly being carried from one district to another on the backs of natives; of its own accord the pest-bearing tsetse fly travels but a short distance. There are great hopes that by means of an aerial photographic survey of these huge forest areas the narrow necks of the forest will be easily located and cuts will be made, thus isolating the fly in his own particular forest area for he always keeps to the shade and will never venture forth into the sunlight.

We were getting into the rainy season now and, having no personal experience of the climatic conditions of the country, I went forward with considerable caution. I think that this section of the route, from about the south end of the Victoria Nyanza to Palapye Road in Bechuanaland, was the worst stretch of our whole flight from London to Cape Town; it was more or less over dense forest the entire way and, except for the prepared landing grounds, for at least 98 per cent of the journey there was nothing but tree-tops on which it would be possible to land a machine.

From Tabora we flew to Abercorn and here came down on a landing ground 5,500 feet above sea level. Abercorn is situated in Northern Rhodesia about 15 miles from the southern end of the great Tanganyika Lake, which, some say is the deepest lake in the world; it is very long and narrow, and soundings have been taken that have registered 3,000 and 4,000 feet. Abercorn is but a mere outpost, situated on a high plateau, where amid beautiful scenery and in a delightful climate it is possible to grow almost anything; on the day of our arrival we indulged in passion fruit, oranges, bananas, apples and strawberries and cream, all of which came from the Commissioner's farm.

Reluctantly we said goodbye to Abercorn and continued on our way to our next landing ground at N'Dola, flying over the great Lake

Tabora.

Bangweolo *en route*, until at last we hit the Northern Rhodesian railway which runs through a rich mineral country right up into the Congo.

Now N'Dola is on the railway line and practically in the heart of a thick forest. My landing grounds in this part of the world, for reasons of economy, were clearings that consisted of two runways 600 yards long and 50 yards wide in the form of a cross, thus making it possible for me to land into four directions of the wind whatever it might be. My original instructions had been that a smoke fire should be lighted immediately the aeroplane was sighted, in order that the drift of the smoke would show me the direction of the wind so that I might land head into it.

It is quite simple to imagine what a terrific landmark a landing ground of this nature must have been in the middle of a thick forest, especially when four great smoke fires were lit at each end of the cross. I believe I could see it twenty miles off, all the more easily because there were special white markings on the runways. One official, however, had many doubts as to whether I should spot the landing ground or not, for soon after we had come down and I had stepped out of the machine, he said to me, 'Could you see the landing ground all right?' Whereupon I replied, 'Perfectly,' and he again remarked 'By gad, when you flew by here in a circle I thought you had missed it, and I tried to attract your attention. Did you see me wave my hat?'

From N'Dola we went southward along the railway line to Broken Hill and from there to Livingstone, where we landed within sight of the Victoria Falls. Here we had one of our greatest adventures of the whole trip.

We had left Broken Hill early in the morning, and after a 300-mile flight southward along the railway line, I could see dimly on the horizon, above the forest, what appeared to be the smoke from two or three fires. But as we got nearer I noticed that this smoke did not drift very much with the wind, and instead of rising continuously it would suddenly disappear and re-appear at another spot a few yards away from its first position. Then gradually it dawned upon me that this was not smoke at all, but clouds of spray rising from the great Victoria Falls.

Presently the River Zambesi could be seen flowing eastwards through the forest, until it took a half-right turn and suddenly disappeared from view; this was where it toppled over the brink of the chasm. We did not trouble to land straight away at Livingstone, although we could see the crowds waiting at our temporary landing ground, but carried on a few miles further to the Falls, aware that this was going to be one of the greatest spectacles of our whole flight.

The Zambesi at this point is well over a mile wide and, as we approached from the north, all that we could see was a long clean-cut line where the river disappeared into the earth, whence huge clouds of spray were continually rising. In a few moments we had flown beyond the brink. I looked behind and had my first glimpse of the vast volume of water, a mile and a quarter long, falling from a height nearly as great as that of the cross of St Paul's Cathedral into a deep chasm from which there is only one small gorge outlet.

My first view of the Falls was perhaps a little disappointing, for from an altitude it is difficult at first to get a real view of the mighty avalanche of water, owing to the fact that it drops into a narrow chasm. The formation of this gorge might be described as that of a T, the Zambesi toppling over the falls into the top line of the T and all the water gushing out down the gorge stem of the T.

The native name of the Falls when translated is 'Smoke Falls', a title inspired by the banks of smoke-like spray which rise night and day from the ravine. These are evidently caused by the great volume of water dragging warm air with it in its mighty drop to the bottom of the gorge; for this continual flow of warm air there is no outlet, as the ravine is hardly fifty yards wide, so it rises again in a terrific up-current on the opposite cliff wall. This constantly rising current of warm air forces the fine spray up in cloudbanks to a height of over 1,000 feet above the brink of the Falls.

We were lucky to arrive just before the flood season, for the spray is then so heavy that it is often impossible to get a view of the cascade. As it was, both Emmott and Elliott were able to take excellent pictures in between the constantly rising banks. Emmott finally wanted to take a real close-up picture of the brink, so I went to the western end and prepared to fly eastward along the edge of the Falls, so that with the sun nicely behind us Emmott might get a perfect forward view from the port window of the cabin. Since the Falls are a mile and a quarter wide, by flying very slowly and taking a long approach, we reckoned that there would be at least two minutes filming to be done.

From about 500 feet we took a picture of the long line of Falls ahead of us; coming lower we got a close-up of the famous Devil's Cataract at the extreme western end, and then continued flying along the Falls about 50 feet above and 50 yards away from the brink. We had been going but a few seconds when suddenly a cloud of spray enveloped us, and although this was only momentary we emerged with

Above: The Victoria Falls
from the air.

Left: The Victoria Falls Gorge.

our wings dripping with water. I looked through the cabin window and noticed that Emmott was turning the handle of his camera with a precision and intentness that I had rarely seen before, for this was the real stuff. A few seconds later, and we were enveloped in another bank of spray, receiving a slight bump as we passed through it. The far end of the brink was almost reached when we flew through a third cloud of fine spray that was denser than all the rest.

At this moment we were directly above the chasm, and only a few feet away on our right loomed the great railway suspension bridge that spans the outlet gorge. On our left were the waters of the Zambesi tumbling over the brink, while ahead were rocky crags with endless forest beyond; so that when at this moment our engine spluttered – cut out for the first time since we had left London – it was naturally a startling experience. She quickly picked up again, but only for a few seconds before further spluttering; by this time, however, we were hundreds of feet above the Falls and steering for our landing ground. At the first falter I had pulled the control lever back, and owing to our enormous reserve of power we had been able to climb quickly.

Our engine continued to splutter, miss and bang, and both Elliott and I knew what had happened. As I looked through the cabin window and saw his somewhat troubled countenance, I shaped the word 'water' with my lips. In flying so close to the brink of the Falls the spray, heavier than we had anticipated, had evidently been sucked through our air-intake pipes into our carburetter. It was imperative to keep the engine running and the propeller turning over so that there might be sufficient momentum to carry the engine on when the globules of water were passing through the jet; that is why we opened full out and climbed as high as possible, until at last we were within gliding distance of our landing ground and knew that we were safe should the water prove too much for the carburation.

By the time we had reached our landing ground the water apparently had been cleared from the carburetter, for we were running quite regularly again and soon had temporarily forgotten our little adventure amid the enthusiasm of our reception by the people of Livingstone. The only person who was not perturbed by the occurrence was Emmott, who seemed oblivious to the fact that anything was wrong, and had been far too busy to worry about engine troubles in the excitement of turning the handle on so thrilling a spectacle. Despite this reassuring attitude, I made a mental note that never again would I fly low over the Victoria Falls and dash through its spray banks in an aeroplane; one felt that with a little more water a submarine would be more suitable for the job.

That afternoon we went down to the Falls on foot and wandered along the cliff on the opposite side of the brink, taking close-up pictures of what we had seen from the air. We wore mackintoshes, and at one spot went close to the edge of the ravine in order to take a picture in a lull between the rising of the banks of spray; but we stayed a moment too long, for a cloud suddenly rose and enveloped us and we found in a few seconds that our mackintoshes were entirely useless. Drenched to the skin, I realised what we had flown

Filming the Rapids above the Falls.

through. We lingered long, taking pictures from every aspect, for the fascination of this mighty waterfall was gripping us, and the rainbow that existed in almost every fresh view we came upon was especially beautiful.

That evening our host suggested that as it was a full moon we should journey once more to the Falls to see the lunar rainbow, a rare sight that occurs only at certain seasons of the year. We motored down on our third visit to the Falls that day and, leaving the car on the roadway, wended our way through a grove of trees to the brink of the cliff at the eastern end of the ravine. There before us was the great silvery grey mass, falling into the dark depths of the gorge, and then as the moon came out from behind a small cloud we had a vision more wonderful than we had seen during the whole day. There appeared what seemed to be the ghost of the rainbow that we had seen in the sunshine. The gentle tinting and colouring of this lunar rainbow had its own mystic charm, and as we all stood gazing in silence upon this beautiful sight I mused over the events of the day and fully realised the foundation and origin of all the native legends

The Zambesi above and below the Falls.

and mystery stories that have been handed down from generation to generation about the great Victoria Falls.

The next stop after Livingstone was Bulawayo, where we received our first really big reception, and I began to realise how important was our task for the good of British aviation and how imperative it was that we should carry the work through successfully. After a busy three days, during which time we visited the famous Matopo Hills and saw Rhodes's grave on World's View, we prepared to take off from our landing ground on the racecourse to fly to Palapye Road and thence on to Pretoria.

Bulawayo is over 4,000 feet above sea level, the day was extremely hot, and unfortunately a very gentle breeze was blowing across the narrow way of the racecourse. My run in this direction was about 350 yards, with trees to clear at the end, and my machine would undoubtedly come off the ground in that distance. But if the aeroplane makes no attempt to leave the ground by the time I still have sufficient room to shut off and pull up within the boundaries of the aerodrome, it has always been my rule not to carry on with the

Rhodes's grave on the Matopo Hills.

take-off but simply to stop the engine and pull up while there is still time.

So, after two attempts, when I felt that the machine was not rising in time, I shut off and came to a standstill within a few yards of the edge of the aerodrome. I felt convinced that the aeroplane would not come off in so short a run with her existing load because, apart from the great altitude of the aerodrome, it was a very hot day, and the atmosphere seemed to be particularly rarefied. Reluctantly I asked Emmott if he would take off his camera gear and baggage, and go along by train to the next stop, and thus lightened we soon bounced off the ground and headed for Palapye Road.

After lunching with the local inhabitants and those who had come scores of miles from the surrounding districts to see our machine, we flew on again into the Union of South Africa to our next stop, the South African Air Force Aerodrome at Pretoria. It struck me very forcibly, after flying for 100 miles south of Palapye Road, how the perpetual forest country suddenly ended and we found ourselves flying over beautiful open rolling plains, with here and there a

Flight engineer
Arthur Elliot
prepares to
hand–crank the
Jaguar into life
at Bulawayo.

43

mountain range and I soon learnt that this type of country, so perfect for aviation, extended right the way to the Cape.

At Pretoria we had an enormous reception, and every facility imaginable was placed at our disposal by Sir Pierre Van Ryneveld, who himself flew from London to Cape Town in 1919. It was here we took the opportunity of the South African Air Force hangars to overhaul our aeroplane, and we were readily assisted by the officers and men of the Air Force.

Johannesburg is only a matter of thirty miles from Pretoria, where they had been eagerly awaiting our arrival for some days. When Sir Pierre Van Ryneveld suggested that we should have an escort of aeroplanes from Pretoria to Johannesburg we all felt very highly honoured, for surely an Air Force could pay a mere civilian expedition no greater compliment. And so it was arranged that before landing at Johannesburg we should fly right along the great gold reef, passing in turn over the various mining towns, where according to previous arrangement the school children had been assembled in their playgrounds to watch the flight.

At Johannesburg we received the greatest reception of all, for over 5,000 people had assembled to witness our arrival, and there were more than 1,000 cars parked on the edge of the landing ground. It was in Johannesburg that our aviation propaganda work started in real earnest it was found necessary for me to employ two secretaries to keep pace with the correspondence, and very often I had to put in eighteen hours a day in order to fulfil all my appointments and complete the work there was to do. Four and five speeches a day were not uncommon, for every society and club wished to hear a few words about aviation and our particular experiences.

From Johannesburg we flew to Kimberley, where at the offices of de Beers we were shown nearly half a million pounds' worth of diamonds displayed on a single counter for sorting, and from Kimberley we went to Bloemfontein, which is the great agriculture marketing town of the Orange Free State. The last lap of the journey took us from Bloemfontein to Beaufort West, where we stayed for lunch,

Arrival at Pretoria; centre, left to right: Sir P. Van Ryneveld; A.B. Elliott; Alan Cobham.

Alan Cobham over Pretoria. Note the Union Buildings in the background and the complete absence of road traffic.

Union Buildings, Pretoria, the administrative seat of the Union of South Africa.

'Topee – or not topee?' That is the question seemingly solved by this colonial welcoming group in South Africa.

LUNCHEON

Given by

MAJOR MILLER, D.S.O. AT THE HOUSE OF ASSEMBLY ON TUESDAY, FEBRUARY 23rd, 1926, TO MR. ALAN COBHAM AND PARTY IN COMMEMORATION OF THEIR FLIGHT FROM LONDON TO CAPE TOWN.

South African air pioneer Major Alastair Miller hosted a farewell luncheon for the Cobham crew just prior to their leaving Cape Town for home.

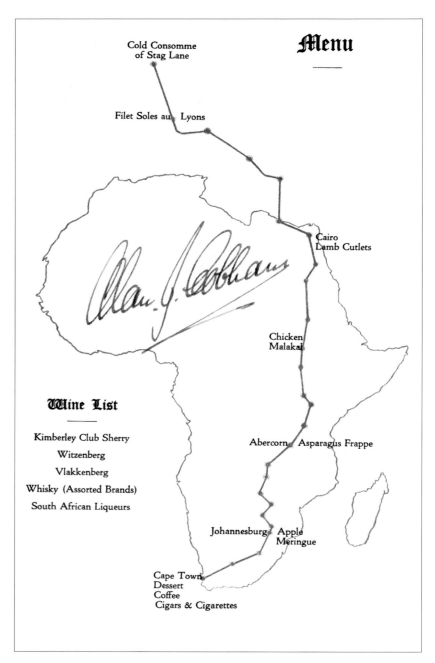

Major Miller's luncheon was the apogee of the social entertaining that engulfed Cobham after his arrival in South Africa.

carrying on afterwards through the Hex River valley, down from our high inland plateau to the lower levels of the Cape Peninsula.

We landed on Wynburg Aerodrome just out of Cape Town and here there was another wonderful reception by the inhabitants of the Peninsula. We had now practically completed the aviation survey that we were making on behalf of the Imperial Airways Company, and we had covered half the distance of our proposed flight. So far our de Havilland aeroplane had stood up to the job perfectly, and our Siddeley Jaguar engine had not given us one moment's anxiety in the air ever since we left London.

CHAPTER III

CAPE TOWN TO LONDON

OUR job of survey over and with a complete knowledge of the route and the allocation of our supplies, we determined to do our utmost to make a speedy flight home, Elliott having overhauled the engine during our stay at Cape Town. It so happened that, on the very day we left, the steamship *Windsor Castle* was sailing for Southampton, and a sort of impromptu race was started in which the competitors were the *Windsor Castle* with Captain Strong 'up', versus the de Havilland aeroplane with Alan Cobham 'up'. The *Windsor Castle* route was one of 5,300 miles, steaming day and night, against ours of 8,500 miles, in which we had to come down at 26 different landing grounds, and as a rule could not do more than eight hours flying a day. So the race was going to be a keen one, and I heard afterwards that much money changed hands in consequence

At 6.45 a.m. on 26 February we were in the air heading for Beaufort West, and after a pleasant passage through the Hex River valley, which is often very bad for flying, we mounted up above the high inland plateau and landed at Beaufort West at about 10 a.m. Here we were met with hot coffee and sandwiches, and so many had sent us baskets of grapes that to carry them all on the machine would have been impossible.

An hour later we departed and made our way towards Kimberley, where we arrived in time for a late lunch, and decided that, owing to the lateness of the hour, it would be impossible to carry on 500

Above: The Union Castle mailship, *Windsor Castle*, failed to beat Cobham's time for the return trip to England.

Left: Captain Strong who commanded the *Windsor Castle*.

miles to our next stop, Palapye Road, and reach there before dark. The night was spent at Kimberley, and the next morning we flew on to Palapye Road, where we refuelled and partook of a hasty lunch, before flying on to Bulawayo.

On this flight we ran into our first real tropical rain storms. We dodged through several and ended up with a race against a heavy storm, striving to reach Bulawayo racecourse and get down on the landing ground before the deluge came. We only just did it, inasmuch as before we could taxi the machine into position, get out of it and take refuge in the grand-stand, the storm burst and drenched us through while we ran for shelter.

The following day we took off from Bulawayo and this time negotiated the job well with maximum full load on board our machine, but even so I discovered that the atmosphere of Rhodesia was particularly rarefied because it took more revolutions of my propeller to make the machine climb and fly level than on any other part of the flight. We passed through continual downpours of rain on our compass course to the railway line below Broken Hill, and on this flight I have vivid recollections of flying in mist and rain over trackless forest and miles of uncharted territory. There were whole ranges of mountains, ravines and rivers of which there was no mark whatsoever on our map – the best that could be procured. Eventually we hit the Rhodesian Railway. The sun began to shine, and as we followed its track to Broken Hill we passed over farmstead after farmstead, at each of which was assembled an enthusiastic and cheering throng. They had heard of our coming, evidently from the rail staff, and had put out flags to cheer us as we passed by. As we flew over a station it would telegraph to the next to say that we were coming, so that those ahead could watch our approach.

We lunched at Broken Hill and, although our host did his utmost to persuade us to stay the night, we carried on again that afternoon to N'Dola. We filled up the machine and went to bed early that night with the intention of getting off at dawn the following morning to fly to Abercorn and thence to Tabora, but the Fates decided otherwise.

In the early hours of the following morning a storm started and five inches of rain fell in the space of four hours. This was too much for our landing ground, and it made the earth so soft that our wheels sank too deep in the mud for us to get up sufficient speed for taking off. We tried time and again, but it was a risky business and we feared that our wheels might suddenly sink too deeply and tip the machine up, so reluctantly we had to postpone our departure to the next day.

The following morning we again tried our luck, but before doing so we enlisted the services of about a thousand natives from the surrounding villages; headed by their leader, these marched *en masse* up and down our fairway, chanting and stamping all the while, with the object of making the ground more solid and – more important still – finding out the weak spots in its surface. We got off safely and headed for Abercorn, and we were all very thankful and pleased with ourselves when, after flying over Lake Bangweolo, we eventually sighted the southern shores of Lake Tanganyika and a little later landed once again on Abercorn Aerodrome.

It was too late to carry on that day to Tabora, so we determined to get up early the following morning and make Kisumu on the equator by the next evening. On our outward flight we had missed the famous Kalombo Falls, which are reported to be the highest in the world. They are formed by a river flowing off the high plateau which exists in south-west Tanganyika and Northern Rhodesia, and falling over a cliff edge into a broad ravine from which the river tumbles down in a mile or so to the extreme south-eastern shore of Lake Tanganyika.

Therefore on our homeward flight we had determined to investigate and photograph these falls, about which so little seemed to be known, although in fact they had been discovered many years ago and had been visited constantly by the various British Commissioners who have been in command at Abercorn. The only feature which recommends these falls is their great height, for it is but a small river that flows over the cliff edge and drops some 700 feet into the ravine. I am told that in the dry season, the river is so small that one can easily walk across it at the brink of the falls, the water never reaches the bottom of the ravine in bulk, but ends up in a spray under which it is possible to walk and not become drenched, providing an umbrella is used.

In due course we found the Falls and did our utmost to get good pictures, but owing to the fact that it was early morning and the sun was low on the horizon, and the Falls face due west, the tumbling water was so much in the shadow that our pictures were hardly successful.

Then we set off on our compass course for Tabora, passing across the great inland plateau and climbing over the escarpment on its eastern edge. Here big cloud banks had formed, and I considered that the best method of keeping my course was to climb above them, much to the delight of Emmott who had a great opportunity taking some really fine cloud pictures.

We landed at Tabora, and just as our machine came to a standstill one wheel sank up to its axle, it took quite a big party of natives to lift us out. Emmott and I quickly filled up when our fuel had been brought down to us; Elliott we left entirely free on the whole of our flight homewards from Cape Town to London to do nothing but inspect and attend to the maintenance of his engine. This was partly

Soft ground at Tabora.

due to the fact that he had contracted malaria fever (we think at Broken Hill, on the outward journey) and had been a whole week in bed during our stay at Johannesburg. Therefore we considered that he was still in a state of convalescence and should not be taxed with any undue form of physical exertion.

When we were ready to depart from Tabora our real difficulties commenced. As we taxied into position to take off, every few yards either one wheel or the other sank deep into the soft earth which had been subject to continual downpours, so we were told, ever since we had departed from Tabora on our outward journey. At last we got into position, and I shall always have recollections of our take off from Tabora as one of the most ghastly performances of the whole flight; as we ran over the aerodrome, with our engine roaring full out in an endeavour to get up flying speed, we ran continually into soft earth and took the risk of tipping up on our nose. However, at last we endeavoured to drag the machine off the ground at a speed which was hardly flying speed, and literally staggered away into the atmosphere.

Once in the air I put the nose down slightly, whereupon our air speed indicator soon jumped up, and we climbed away with ease.

We reached Kisumu that night, having flown 700 miles in the day, and the following morning set off on a 450-mile trip to Mongalla in the Sudan. It was not until we got within about fifty miles of Mongalla and started to come down from our high altitude that we really began to feel the heat, and when about noon we landed on the aerodrome at Mongalla, it was like coming suddenly into a furnace. To eat was impossible, and after several long drinks we set about the task of filling up again, for we had determined to do another 360-mile jump to Malakal that day

Despite the heat, we took off from Mongalla very quickly with a full load on board and headed northward, climbing hard for Malakal. The heat was the greatest that we had experienced on our whole flight for the wind on the ground had been burning hot before we started, and as the day progressed so the atmosphere seemed to warm up. By the time our engine had climbed to 5,000 feet its lubricating oil was beginning to get a bit warm, but this did not matter much so long as we could maintain our oil pressure. It was lucky that we had supplies of Castrol Oil, because I know of no other that would have stood such temperatures.

There were moments when it was impossible to put one's face over the side of the aeroplane because the draught was like a hot flame. This was at 5,000 feet, and I found that by going up another 1,500 feet we reached a cooler atmosphere. So, flying at an altitude of nearly 7,000 feet, we passed over the dried up plains east of the Sud area, until we came again to Malakal. I think that the coming down from our high altitude was the most trying experience of all, because it gave us the impression of descending into a kind of oven, and we felt that if we went much lower it would be impossible to breathe.

Although the heat on the ground was very trying, it was not intensified by the rush of hot wind on one's face as in the air.

After spending the night at Malakal we flew on the following day to Khartoum, where we had originally intended to refuel quickly and carry on to Wadi Haifa, 700 miles further. But despite the fact that the Air Force fellows had our cases of B.P. spirit out on the aeroplane all ready for refuelling, owing to the enormous distance that we had covered in the last two or three days, we all felt too tired to carry on; besides, there was hardly time to reach our destination before dark. At Khartoum we met the Cairo-Cape RAF Flight and we were happy to augment, from our own experiences, their information concerning the route ahead of them.

That night a bad sandstorm blew from the north, and we heard that at Abu Hamed, halfway between Khartoum and Wadi Haifa, a *haboob* was raging. This went on through the evening and into the night. With the worst of the storm over, we took off from Khartoum on the following morning and started to climb through dust-laden air; at 5,000 feet we were still in the sandstorm, and so climbed on until at 11,000 feet we were not completely out of the dust for there were still banks of fine sand floating above us at that altitude.

As we flew our visibility was nil, except when we looked immediately beneath us and could dimly see, passing across the yellow sand some 10,000 feet below, a broad dark shadow that was the Nile.

We landed at Atbara after descending through the yellow coloured atmosphere, and learnt from the railway officials that the dust would be worse ahead; but they advised us to go on as next day there might be another *haboob*. Again we climbed, this time to nearly 12,000 feet, and the further north we flew the more difficult it became to distinguish the river beneath. This was our only guide, for it was unsafe to go on a compass course, because if the weather became too bad and forced us to land in the desert, we should be lost and never found.

Suddenly I discovered that the dim shadow I was following on the ground was not the River Nile, and at 12,000 feet in an awful moment I realised that we were for the time lost. Ahead and around us were yellow banks of dust clouds, and beneath we could dimly discern the earth which was the desert. A few moments previously I felt positive that I had seen the river below to the west, so I dived earthwards to find it. Minutes passed and many miles were covered as we dived down and down in search of our only hope. When at last we were within but a few hundred feet of the ground and still no Nile was in sight, the terrible calamity of the situation dawned upon me; it was impossible to know which way to fly to reach habitation or life of any sort, it was useless to fly on and hopeless for us to land. At this moment luckily I spotted an old dried-up waterway such as one sees in the desert. Ascertaining which way the ancient flow had been, I followed the dry river bed downwards for a few minutes, which seemed like hours, when suddenly the Nile came into view.

After this experience, dust or no dust, we flew twenty feet above the railway line to make sure of keeping it in sight, the river and railway here running side by side. As we neared Abu Hamed the dust became thicker, but our engine ran perfectly in spite of it. Eventually we left the river, and at twenty feet above and a few yards to the right of the telegraph poles, we skimmed through the dust-laden air over the perfectly flat, reliefless yellow desert, following the railway northwards to

Wadi Haifa. It was necessary to concentrate on the railway line, for the open desert seemed to merge into the atmosphere so that there was no horizon and one could not tell which was desert and which was dust storm, and the railway line was the only guide.

At last we left the windings of the Nile and followed the almost dead straight railway into the desert for hundreds of miles. Skimming along within a few feet of the earth at 110 miles per hour became extremely fatiguing, and instinctively we throttled back and went slower so that the telegraph poles did not flyby so quickly in a bewildering blur.

In the cabin I noticed that Elliott was quietly writing up engine log books and at intervals pumping petrol up, while Emmott amused himself by turning the handle of his beloved camera on the fast passing railway track. At last we arrived at Wadi Haifa, refuelled and flew up the Nile in slightly better weather to Assuan.

There was a head wind, and as the sun sank into the dust-laden air I knew that the sunset would be earlier than usual; low over the waters of the Nile, we raced along to get in before dark, and at last we reached beautiful Assuan with our day's journey over, all three somewhat tired after our trying experience.

On Sunday we took off on the last lap of our flight to Cairo and passed over the old and familiar sites of Thebes, Luxor, Karnak and Assuit. We had a cross wind on the first half of the journey, but later the wind got behind us and we covered the four hundred and eighty miles in four hours forty minutes, the Pyramids of Giza coming into view sooner than we expected. On landing at Heliopolis we were given a hearty reception by the RAF, among whom was Air Vice-Marshal Sir Oliver Swann. A few moments after we had landed the Air Mail came in from Baghdad, having been delayed by the wind that had helped us.

We had been successful in accomplishing the flight from the Cape to Cairo for the first time in history, and we had taken nine days to do it.

I believe that had not the tropical rains detained us at N'Dola and lost us more time at Abercorn, and if the heat of the Sudan had not been quite so great, we should have made the journey with ease in six days.

On the following morning we were all in readiness to depart for Sollum in an endeavour to make Athens that day, but it was practically impossible to start as a gale was blowing at fifty miles an hour from the south-west. Under such circumstances we could not reach Sollum, 400 miles away, on our petrol capacity of only six hours. Reluctantly we waited at Cairo, filling in the time in clearing up, with the assistance of the RAF, many little business affairs that might have been neglected had we pushed straight on.

The next morning we reached Sollum by 10 a.m., and filled up quickly in readiness to set out across the Mediterranean and make Athens that night. We had started our engine up and were taxying into position over the rocky surface of the landing ground, when our tail skid became caught in a stubborn rock and broke. The damage was fairly serious since it would take longer than a few moments to repair and our chances of reaching Athens that day were ended.

We cursed, but had to content ourselves with the prospects of an early start the following day. The afternoon was spent in repairing the tail skid, then we took our machine over the frontier to an Italian 'drome where there was a hangar, because the Wing Commander of an RAF flight that was stranded on Sollum told us that our little machine would be blown away if left in the open on their landing ground.

The following day a terrific gale blew from the north, again making it impossible for us to reach our destination on our petrol capacity. I feared that the head wind might blow for days in this direction, and so decided that at all costs we must fly against it on the morrow. Therefore we had to increase our petrol capacity to make up for possible slow progress. All the camera gear, many spare parts and a lot of baggage were taken off the DH50 and shipped back to Cairo, to be forwarded home. Having lightened the machine in this way, we took on board ten four-gallon cans of extra petrol. These cans so completely filled the cabin that I hardly knew how Elliott and Emmott were going to refuel during the flight into tanks inside the cabin.

With our colossal load on board we got off well and headed out northwards for the open Mediterranean; very soon we were out of sight of land, for here the visibility was unusually poor. During our long flight over the water Elliott and Emmott were kept busy in the cabin, struggling and juggling with petrol cans which they had to empty through an improvised hole in one of the cabin petrol tanks. In the ordinary course of events we should have seen land about two hours after losing sight of the African coast, so when there was still no sight of land after three hours flight we naturally began to think a little. I stuck to my compass course because I knew that, even if drift had lessened or increased, I must surely hit either the eastern end of Crete or on the other hand the mainland of Greece.

Visibility was very bad; whereas it had been possible to see for twenty or thirty miles on other occasions that I had crossed this part of the Mediterranean now we could not see more than a mile ahead. Three and a half hours had passed and still there was no sight of land, but we carried on through rainstorm after rainstorm and became a little anxious, having come so far on a dead reckoning that we began to doubt our approximate whereabouts. Perhaps our imaginations set to work at this time, for I began to wonder whether I had allowed enough degrees to rectify my drift, and whether possibly we might be going up into the Ægean Sea beyond the eastern end of the Island of Crete. On the other hand, I might have exaggerated grossly the strength of the west wind and allowed too much for drift, so that we might be missing the mainland of Greece and flying on into the open Ionian Sea.

We were endeavouring to make Cape Krio at the extreme south-west corner of Crete. Repeatedly we saw shadows on the water and, the wish being father to the thought they were constantly mistaken for land. At last, however, I saw dimly the real thing about a mile away to the east, and on flying towards it very soon discerned a steep and rocky coastline. It was a great relief to all of us. As we neared these mountains that seemed to rise sheer out of the sea, I realised that it was not the corner of Crete and a little later, by locating another island away to the north, discovered that the land that we had sighted was the isle of Cythera. Thus our compass course had been a good one, but, owing to the very bad visibility, we had flown within a few miles of the islands of Gaudo and Gaudo Pula, Cape Krio and the island of Cerigotto without seeing them. Had the day been fine we should have sighted our first island from quite a long way off, and with a slight alteration of our compass bearing picked up the corner of Crete.

Very soon we struck the mainland of Greece and had to fly a little way due east with the wind behind us in order to round Cape Malea before heading northward for Athens. There was a strong westerly gale blowing, and, as I was flying down wind with the gale that was coming straight from the sea, I was in a comparatively calm atmosphere and forgot for the moment that the gale was blowing. However, the moment we rounded the Cape within a few hundred yards of the cliffs and flew northwards, we came into the violent down currents off the mountains. I can say without hesitation that although in the past I have had some very bad experiences, due to down currents from mountains, especially along the Mediterranean coastline, on this occasion it was my worst experience to date. First of all we were bumped about violently in all directions for a minute or so, and then suddenly we were caught in one terrific down current, falling so fast that the passengers and all the baggage were literally pressed tight against the roof of the cabin. So long did this down-current continue that the petrol in the top tank was evidently forced up against its roof. Our petrol system was gravity fed and, as we were falling faster than gravity could pull our fuel down the pipe, the engine was starved and she cut out.

As we neared the water there was a sudden up-pressure, for our downward course had an abrupt check whereupon the engine started running again and, amid many more bumps, I lost no time in heading for the open sea. A few minutes later we were some miles

Athens from the Air with the stadium visible in the foreground.

from the shore and flying in a comparatively calm atmosphere. It had been a somewhat severe lesson to me not to get too near the leeward side of the mountains when a gale is blowing over them. Possibly I should have surmised what would happen, but owing to the bad visibility I was not fully aware of the vast mountains and general physical formation of the country; otherwise our disturbing experience could have been avoided.

As a result of this flight we had the satisfaction of gaining an experience which showed us that the best plan for a commercial air line round the coast of the Mediterranean would be by seaplane flying well out to sea.

We arrived at Athens in sunshine after a trip of 480 miles over the water from Africa, all of us having a little pride in the fact that, although the trip had been done many times with the prevailing following winds from Athens to Africa, we were the first people in history to fly against a head wind from Africa to Athens.

From Athens we intended to make a final dash home, so we rose in the darkness long before dawn and motored out to Tatoi aerodrome in an icy morning air, which we all felt extremely after the heat of the Sudan. We then flew 360 miles to Taranto at the heel of Italy, filled tip, enjoyed an alfresco lunch and made another 500 miles to Pisa. The next morning we were up early again with the intention of flying via the Riviera coastline to Lyons, but on account of perfect weather conditions I decided to cross the Alps by way of Turin and the Modane Pass. Our passage over the Alps was probably one of the most beautiful flights of the whole trip and, whereas it would have been possible to clear the Pass at 8,000 feet, we cruised over in the wonderful clear morning air at 12,000 feet, surrounded on all sides by the hundreds of glistening snow-covered peaks of the Alps.

We landed at Lyons and after refuelling, dispatching wires, and partaking of coffee and rolls, we set off on the last lap of our 17,000 mile journey. The flight from Lyons to London is about 480 miles, I had to push the engine a little because we encountered a somewhat contrary wind, and I wished to arrive at Croydon at 4 p.m. as I had telegraphed. We flew low over Paris, crossed the Channel, and

A restless crowd prepare to engulf the DH50 (extreme right) as it taxies past Vickers Vulcan G-EBLB of Imperial Airways.

Cobham touches down at Croydon on 13 March 1926.

Cobham arrives at Croydon to a tumultuous welcome from crowds seemingly
oblivious to the whirling propeller.

'Would you sign, please?' Cobham considered his end of journey fatigue due as much to autograph hunters as the flight itself.

then at Sevenoaks were met by a whole host of aeroplanes in the air. There were six Moth machines and in one Mrs Cobham, piloted by Capt. de Havilland, had come out to meet us. Very soon a formation was formed about us and thus we arrived at Croydon.

We were all surprised and somewhat overwhelmed at the reception we received, and it seemed that we should never be able to get away from the aerodrome again. I had a letter on board the machine from the Earl of Athlone, Governor and Commander-in-Chief of the Union of South Africa, addressed to His Majesty the King. I enquired how and when I should deliver this letter, and soon received instructions to go to Buckingham Palace as quickly as possible.

A few moments later, accompanied by Mrs Cobham, I flew our machine over London back to its home at Stag Lane, put it away in the hangar, jumped into a waiting car and went straightaway to

The sand-blasted DH50J provides a crowd-pulling exhibit at Selfridges' London store.

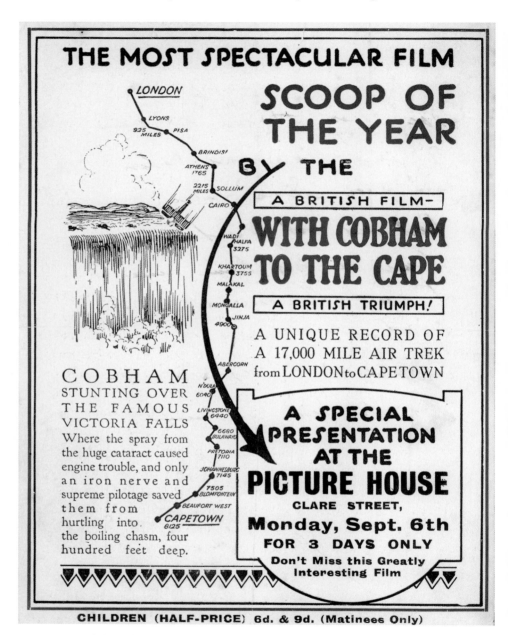

Emmott's film of the journey proved to be an enormous success and netted some £8,000 profit for Cobham. The publicity department appear to have overhyped Cobham's heart-stopping moment over Victoria Falls, however, for he never engaged in 'stunting'!

Buckingham Palace. I soon discovered how keen was His Majesty on the subject of aviation, for after congratulating me on our success, he asked me many questions regarding our experiences, and I was surprised to find what a keen insight he had into our flight. After I had delivered the letter, Mrs Cobham was presented, and then we hastened on to the broadcasting station.

By 11 p.m. our day's job was finished, and it had been a very long one indeed. Rising at 4 a.m. that morning at Pisa, we had flown nearly 900 miles during a day that had been very eventful, even when the flying was finished.

In conclusion let me say that we all felt that the flight from London to Cape Town and back had been worth while. Emmott was satisfied that he had a picture which the Gaumont Company would have no difficult in getting the renters to take up, for he thought that it would give the public a vivid idea of our experiences. Elliott was happy because the Siddeley Jaguar engine had proved a huge success, and we had not had the slightest suggestion of engine failure, while the de Havilland aeroplane was as good as when it started. Personally I was content that my report on aviation possibilities between London and Cape Town and my report on the behaviour of the machine and engine would be of great use to British aviation at large, and that from a propaganda point of view our flight had been a success.

I would take this opportunity of thanking the Air Ministry for valuable help and of expressing my gratitude to all those enterprising firms who came forward and financed the expedition, as well as to the companies and individuals throughout the route from London to Cape Town who willingly assisted us to complete our flight successfully.

AUSTRALIA AND BACK

Reproduced by kind permission of Lady Cobham.

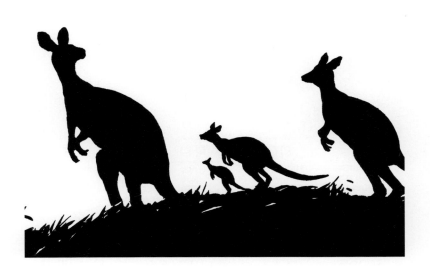

Cobham's journey to Australia (solid line) and return 30 June–1 October 1926. (Courtesy of Airways)

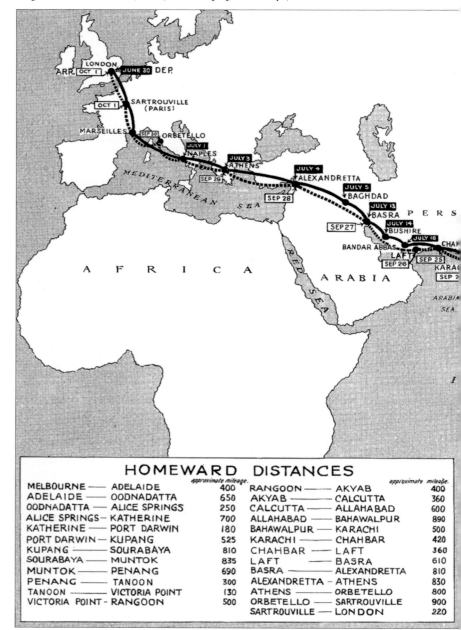

HOMEWARD DISTANCES

		approximate mileage			approximate mileage
MELBOURNE —— ADELAIDE		400	RANGOON —— AKYAB		400
ADELAIDE —— OODNADATTA		650	AKYAB —— CALCUTTA		360
OODNADATTA —— ALICE SPRINGS		250	CALCUTTA —— ALLAHABAD		600
ALICE SPRINGS – KATHERINE		700	ALLAHABAD —— BAHAWALPUR		890
KATHERINE —— PORT DARWIN		180	BAHAWALPUR —— KARACHI		500
PORT DARWIN – KUPANG		525	KARACHI —— CHAHBAR		420
KUPANG —— SOURABAYA		810	CHAHBAR —— LAFT		360
SOURABAYA —— MUNTOK		835	LAFT —— BASRA		610
MUNTOK —— PENANG		690	BASRA —— ALEXANDRETTA		810
PENANG —— TANOON		300	ALEXANDRETTA – ATHENS		830
TANOON —— VICTORIA POINT		130	ATHENS —— ORBETELLO		800
VICTORIA POINT – RANGOON		500	ORBETELLO —— SARTROUVILLE		900
			SARTROUVILLE —— LONDON		220

OUTWARD DISTANCES

approximate mileage

LONDON	NAPLES	1,130	RANGOON	VICTORIA POINT	550
NAPLES	ATHENS	650	VICTORIA POINT	PENANG	400
ATHENS	ALEXANDRETTA	760	PENANG	SINGAPORE	420
ALEXANDRETTA	BAGHDAD	460	SINGAPORE	MUNTOK	270
BAGHDAD	BASRA	300	MUNTOK	BATAVIA	370
BASRA	BUSHIRE	250	BATAVIA	SOURABAYA	465
BUSHIRE	BANDAR ABBAS	400	SOURABAYA	BIMA	435
BANDAR ABBAS	KARACHI	740	BIMA	KUPANG	400
KARACHI	BAHAWALPUR	500	KUPANG	PORT DARWIN	525
BAHAWALPUR	DELHI	500	PORT DARWIN	NEWCASTLE WATERS	380
DELHI	ALLAHABAD	400	NEWCASTLE WATERS	CAMOOWEAL	350
ALLAHABAD	CALCUTTA	550	CAMOOWEAL	CHARLEVILLE	750
CALCUTTA	AKYAB	360	CHARLEVILLE	SYDNEY	840
AKYAB	RANGOON	400	SYDNEY	MELBOURNE	450

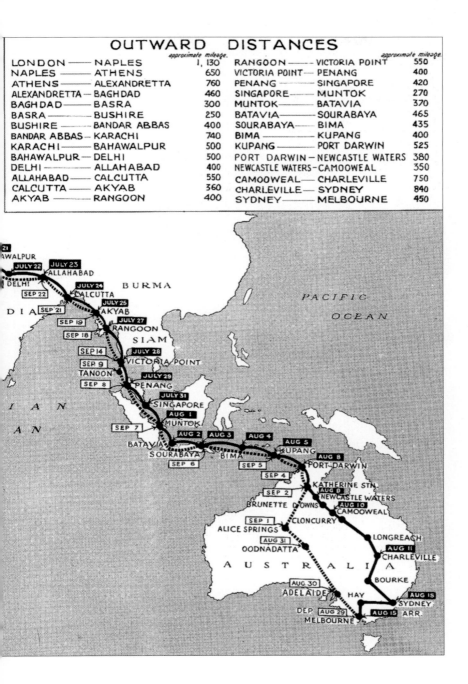

73

Arthur Elliott, Lord Wakefield and Alan Cobham at Short Brothers' Rochester factory just prior to departure.

FOREWORD

Though I accede with very great pleasure to Sir Alan Cobham's request that I should write a foreword to his book, I feel that neither his great exploit itself nor his own vivid and fascinating account of it needs any introduction to British people. I remember the absorbed interest of the Australian people in his outward flight; the painful anxiety with which they read of the tragic fate of his mechanic Elliott; the relief they felt as he surmounted one obstacle after another in the latter stages of the journey; the enthusiasm of their greeting on his arrival among them; and the pride and satisfaction occasioned in their minds by his successful return flight. I have no doubt that all these feelings were shared in like measure by the people of Britain, and Sir Alan Cobham has the satisfaction of knowing that his splendid feat was recognised immediately at its true worth by every citizen of the Empire. It was apparent, too, that the success of the flight against adverse conditions of every kind was not only evidence of the airman's personal courage, but also convincing proof that aerial communication between Britain and Australia throughout the year was perfectly feasible, given the requisite preparation.

There is therefore little need at this late date for me, or for anyone else, to dwell upon the true meaning of this young pioneer's accomplishment, or of its value to the cause of Empire unity. That would be to tell a thrice-told tale. Nor need I reiterate the point that he has demonstrated to the world that the spirit of Drake and Raleigh, of Franklin and Livingstone, lives still in the modern world. Science, if it has added to our comfort and softened the material basis of our lives, has also opened new fields for conquest by the eternal spirit of youth and high endeavour. For this evidence that the old qualities of the British race remain unimpaired in the hearts of the Empire's best sons, I offer him, in my own name and in the name of all his fellow-citizens, thanks and homage.

S.M. Bruce
Prime Minister of Australia
11 November 1926

CHAPTER I

ROCHESTER TO BASRA

Familiar as I may be with long-distance flights around the world, the idea of flying from England to Australia and back with a seaplane seemed to offer a new little adventure – something different to anything that I had attempted before. The reason for taking a seaplane on this flight was chiefly one of protection, because we had decided to fly right through the heart of the monsoon in India and Burma, both on the outward and return trips, and from my previous experience over these countries, when piloting Sir Sefton Brancker to Rangoon and back, I knew how difficult the country would be with an aeroplane. From Calcutta to Australia it is simply impossible to land anywhere but on a specially prepared aerodrome. I did not like to contemplate being caught out in a severe monsoon storm over such country – over tropical jungle, with no prospects of landing – and so decided that although a sea plane has many disadvantages as compared with an aeroplane, it would certainly be a far more practical and safe proposition.

I knew that the coast line of Burma and Malay abounded in sheltered bays and inland creeks and in these I imagined I could take refuge if a severe monsoon storm should overtake me.

I have always maintained that a flight of this nature is half accomplished on the day we start from home, for the success of a flight does not merely depend, as most people imagine, on the trivial matter of handling the control lever and rudder bar in the pilot's cockpit.

I would say that the actual piloting is just about fifteen to twenty per cent of the job, while the backbone of the successful flight is the ground organisation that is put in before the flight is commenced and throughout the journey.

After the return from the Cape flight I set to work immediately to organise our flight to Australia, but before even the most elementary organisation could be put down I had to satisfy those who were going to help in my scheme that I had sound financial backing. The finding of finance is no easy business, for no matter how heartily people may congratulate one on the success of a former flight, so many of these same people can readily find an excuse for being unable to support one financially on the next flight, and so there was a severe uphill task to get the backing for this enterprise. But after the first few promises I set to work to get people interested all along the route.

It must be remembered that ninety in every hundred we met at the various landing-places between London and Australia had never seen a seaplane before, and even a greater percentage than this knew little or nothing about aircraft and what was required for the safe landing, mooring-up and taking off again of a seaplane. Therefore I had to depend entirely upon the willingness of the various authorities at the landing-places I chose on the map, to put down moorings and attend to my requirements from instructions and information which I gave them by letter and cable. So that the entire organisation of the flight was done by cable and correspondence. This meant a tremendous amount of work, and as there were piles of letters to attend to in the clearing up of the Cape flight, I found myself in a somewhat exhausted condition by the time we were finally ready to start on the Australian venture some three months later.

After postponing the date of our departure three times for various reasons, on a fine morning on the last day of June I was called at 4 a.m., as we were going to endeavour to fly from Rochester to Naples in the day. I had said goodbye to my wife the day before and had motored down in the late afternoon to Rochester and slept the night at the 'Bull' hotel, well-known to Dickens readers. Getting up in the dark was never my strong point, but I knew that if we wished to get a move on with the flight before us I should have to acquire the habit, because the early hours in the heat of the tropics are the best for flying. I was greatly surprised when I arrived at Short's works to find that a merry little party of my friends had motored down through the night from London to see me off and to my joy my wife, instead of going to bed, had sat up with a party at home and then motored down with them to Rochester.

There was not a breath of wind to help our get-off and the water was dead calm, but somehow we managed to get unstuck and by 5 a.m. we were in the air, waving goodbye to the sporting little crowd who had turned out to see us off. So many of my friends seemed shocked at the idea of flying across France in a seaplane. Personally I fail to see how this was an extraordinary prospect, because it would be possible to land on various rivers such as the Seine and

Cobham and Arthur Elliott in pre-flight preparation at Short Brothers' Rochester factory.

the Rhone, and even had we been forced to come down on land I do not think that we should have been in great danger of personal injury, although we might have ruined our floats. On the other hand my friends would not have been in the least disturbed had I contemplated flying with an aeroplane miles along the Mediterranean coast line, where it would have been impossible to land the machine along the rocky shores except in the sea itself, which would have meant a complete 'write-off' to the aircraft and a most unpleasant experience for the personnel.

When I left Rochester I was very happy to think that I had a pair of floats beneath me, as the majority of the route from England to Australia would be along coast lines, over the sea, or above rivers. Soon after leaving Rochester we passed over Maidstone, for we were on a direct compass course to Rouen, and as we left the shores of England in the region of Hastings and passed out over the Channel I had a feeling of safety and contentment such as I had never experienced before when flying over the Channel. I was not a seaplane pilot and, with the exception of about four trial flights during the week previous to our departure, I had never flown a sea-plane before; likewise Elliott, my engineer who had accompanied me on so many flights, including the one to Rangoon and back and the one to the Cape and back, knew little or nothing about seaplanes. However, I was convinced that a seaplane was the correct craft in which to fly to Australia and, despite all the discouragement I received regarding the difficulties of handling a seaplane, I decided, in view of my intimate knowledge of many seaplane experts, that the difficulties were exaggerated and that I should find no really great difficulty in managing a hydroplane.

Before going further with the story I must explain that the maximum permissible load of the de Havilland 50 aeroplane is four thousand two hundred pounds, but owing to the extra weight of floats and the additional petrol and equipment necessary for this flight, my maximum load was now in the region of five thousand pounds. Despite this thousand-pound over-load the machine not only got off well but flew perfectly the whole time.

After about forty minutes flying, the coast of France came into view and then we continued our course until we hit Rouen, where we turned south-east, flying along the course of the Seine towards Sartrouville, a French seaplane base on the Seine north of Paris. It had been arranged that we should land here to refill and then continue our journey on to Marseilles, but as my machine carried about one hundred and fifty gallons of petrol, which should have been sufficient for a safe seven and a half hours' flying, I estimated that with favourable winds I ought to be able to reach Marseilles non-stop on my petrol capacity if I cruised at about one hundred miles per hour. At this speed our petrol consumption with the Siddeley-Jaguar engine was about eighteen gallons an hour, and although on paper the 670-mile journey from Rochester to Marseilles looked quite safe with a big margin of petrol, in reality there was none too big a margin, especially if we met with a head wind. Therefore all the way from Rouen to Paris I was trying to calculate on the writing pad in my cock-pit whether or not I could pass over Sartrouville without landing to refill, and was endeavouring to do simple proportion sums on the lines of 'If I can do 220 miles in so many minutes, how long will it take to do 670 miles? etc., etc.' Finally I decided that I would carry on, as it was fairly certain that the gentle north-west wind would prevail throughout the flight and I should reach Marseilles in good order. We passed over Sartrouville, over Paris and down the Seine towards Fontainebleau, and then over open country down the Loire for hundreds of miles until we came to St Etienne. All along this route I was looking ahead to see if heavy cloud-banks were forming; because these would have made the crossing of the mountains over into the Rhone valley somewhat difficult. However, it was a perfect day; the country beneath looked simply delightful, and at 4,500 feet we passed round Mont Pilat and flew down into the Rhone valley.

I have always noticed in the past that atmosphere and climate change suddenly south of the gorge of the Rhone and about eighty miles north of the Mediterranean. The variable, misty, cold weather of northern Europe suddenly ceases and one breaks into a beautiful warm, clear, sunny atmosphere. We landed at Marseilles after six hours and forty minutes' non-stop flight from Rochester, and came to rest on a perfectly ideal seaplane base, the Berre Lake, on whose shores the aerodrome of Marignane has been built, thus forming a perfect combined seaplane and aeroplane base. The lake was ideal because there was no current and no tide, and yet a fair breeze blowing to assist one in the get-off and to avoid a dead calm water. We soon came alongside the jetty and were ready to fill up immediately, because we still had to contemplate another 450-mile flight to Naples, but we were dismayed to discover that our petrol was stored at least two miles away! It is true that they were not quite sure of the time of our arrival, although they knew we were coming, but at the same time I cannot imagine why petrol for a seaplane should be stored two miles or more away from the base. However this little difficulty was soon overcome, and after a small delay we were in the process of filling up. Curiously, for the first time in my experience I was not enthusiastic about my new venture and from the moment of starting I was miserably depressed – possibly homesick – and suffering from both mental and physical exhaustion. Perhaps we had overworked ourselves in the preparation of the flight, although we had always done that in the past and generally started our ventures on the verge of a nervous breakdown, depending upon the exhilaration of flying away into new atmospheres to pull us together and renew our vitality. After a hasty cup of coffee, roll and butter and some cheese, we left our kind friends at Marseilles and taxied out into the open lake and took off.

There was a feeling of security in the new order of things when we opened out and simply headed into the air with no worry about the boundaries of the aerodrome or holes that might be in its surface, or the fact that the tyre might burst, or that we must get off the ground before we came to the rough part, and that telegraph wires had to be cleared at the far end, and such like little distractions that have to be considered when taking off from the average aerodrome.

Instead we had miles of open rippling blue water before us, and with no worry at all we just opened out and away, until the machine had gathered up sufficient headway to lift her on to the first step of the floats and then gradually, as we gathered speed, we had ample time to ease the control lever gently back and lift the craft smoothly off the water, and so on into the air and away upon the new journey.

Our course from Marseilles to Naples lay via the Straits of Bonifacio between Corsica and Sardinia and then on straight over the sea again to the Italian coast. In the past my trips along the Mediterranean had always been round the coast of the Riviera by way of Genoa and Spezia to Pisa, where one always ran the risk of meeting severe bumps, especially if a northerly wind was blowing off the Alps. But now we were going to make a direct cut across the open sea and, as I have always found, no matter how strong the wind may be blowing, violent bumps are rarely met when one is well away from the land. There was no difficulty in hitting upon Corsica or finding our way between the two islands, but as we left Corsica and Sardinia behind us on the port and starboard there was a little worry as to whether we should arrive at Naples before dark. Continually we kept looking behind to see how high the sun was in the sky and then again at our watches to check up how much more daylight we were supposed to have. Then again I started calculating on my writing pad, after measuring up in a most inaccurate manner with my fingers on the map the distance that I had to run.

One drawback in flying from west to east on a long flight is that one loses daylight each day to the extent of about one hour per thousand miles throughout the whole flight. The time question was always muddling because, apart from the fact that sun-time was naturally different at every place we landed, each town or country had its own local time, and then again some had special summer time, and between the lot one could easily be misled. I quickly discovered that the only way to be safe was to ascertain from my official documents exactly how much daylight existed in each particular latitude and then make a note of the time at which the sun rose. From that I could judge the time at which it was going to set by my own watch. We floated into Naples about half an hour before dark, for the sun had already gone down.

The seaplane base at Naples is on the mainland side of the little island of Nisida, which is nothing more than a giant rock towering up out of the water about three hundred yards from the mainland. On the top of this rock a prison was built centuries ago and it has always been considered a stronghold and now on the leeward side of this little island they have built a seaplane base. I had been warned before leaving London of telegraph wires that run from the island to the mainland, but even so I only missed them by a matter of a few feet, because in the dim light of the evening it was impossible to distinguish these wires which were literally hundreds of feet in the air and right in the main fairway of any aircraft coming in to land on the sheltered waters. In fact they would have made a perfect trap in war-time if bait had been put down in the harbour to entice enemy machines.

The moment we landed, our Italian friends came out in a motor launch and took us in tow and immediately started to make preparations for our re-fuelling. Elliott and I were out to put up as good a show as possible, and although we were very tired and had completed the journey from London to Naples in a day for the first time in history, we began to get filled up immediately with the aid of a lamp, by the usual antiquated and obsolete method of pouring petrol out of cans through a hole in the tank. I have often thought how aircraft designers struggle with great aerodynamical problems both in design and construction to obtain possibly one or two miles an hour extra speed out of an aeroplane; this extra bit of speed is generally accomplished with much sacrifice and expense in cost of production, and finally brings a machine into port twenty minutes sooner, then through inefficient, primitive filling-up methods hours will be wasted in re-fuelling. And yet any third-rate engineer could think out a practical and simple device that could fill even the biggest of tanks in the matter of a few minutes.

Refuelling was a lengthy process and often required chamois leather filtering when petrol was supplied from dubious sources.

In a somewhat exhausted condition we stepped aboard the little rowing boat and went ashore on the island for a few moments while I signed up for the petrol received, and then readily acceded to the advice of my agent to go over to the mainland to have some dinner. We were soon in a little pinnace speeding across the bay to a small restaurant on a pier which jutted out over the beach, whose lamps we could see in the distance. The sky was full of stars, but somehow I could not enjoy the situation. It is true we both felt a little faint from our day's exertions and lack of food, but on top of it all I was depressed and could not understand why. However, we were thirsty – very thirsty – and rather disgusted when they offered us heavy red wine to quench the said thirst, but we soon diluted it with plenty of soda-water, ate our meal, and then motored up into the town of Naples for the night.

Our host took us to his apartment, which was a very spacious one, being the top flat of a converted ancient palace whose foundations are washed by the waters of the Mediterranean. Before going to bed we looked out of our lofty windows right over the Bay of Naples. Elliott was cheerful and full of the spirit of adventure. I, on the other hand, was simply exhausted, and amid these wonderful surroundings could only find it in my heart to regret that I should have to be up before dawn next morning, ready to push on with the next stage of our flight to Athens. I felt I wanted to linger for some unknown reason; I had no spirit left in me with which to contemplate the thirteen thousand odd miles that separated us from Melbourne. Our kind host, as he promised, wakened us the following morning at 4.30, but to my dismay I found that I was in no condition to carry on. I had a bad head and felt so weak that I hardly deemed it advisable to get up, although by about six o'clock I had mustered sufficient energy to dress. In this rather shaky condition I journeyed in the car down to Nisida Island. There were one or two minor engine adjustments to attend to, and as we had wasted a certain amount of valuable time I decided that I would rest until about eleven o'clock and content myself with making Athens only that day, instead of the double jump to the Island of Leros as originally planned.

I have always noticed that in Italy the weather is either very good or very bad. By that I mean either clear blue skies, warm sunshine and gentle breezes, or heavy overcast skies, half a gale blowing, bumpy atmosphere and a general liability to storm. It was under the latter conditions that we took off from Nisida Island. The seaplane base there is not a good one, because with the wind in the wrong direction the water can be so rough that even a boat at anchor could hardly live in it, let alone a seaplane, and so when we finally took off at about noon I had to make up my mind to get unstuck very quickly before I reached the breakers of the open sea. We were fortunate in getting up speed quickly, and although we skimmed over the tops of three or four big breakers, hitting them with an unpleasant thud, we were soon in the air and speeding on over the Bay of Naples towards Capri. We could see the island dimly through the mist and in my mind I compared the view ahead with the picture that I remembered of Capri on other occasions. We flew right on down the rocky coast of Italy until we came to Cetraro on that narrow neck of land – the instep – and here I determined to cross the mountains if possible and thus cut in half the great circular tour that would be necessary if we flew right round the Straits of Messina. Our cut over the land necessitated climbing to about five thousand feet and now I experienced the joys of piloting a well-built machine. For although our de Havilland 50 fitted as a sea plane was distinctly overloaded for our wing section when full tanks and all spares were on board, yet the Siddeley Jaguar engine with its 385 horse-power gave us plenty of pull. We soon climbed over the rocky heights and came down into the Gulf of Taranto on the other side. After this we ran into some very heavy rain and drizzle, but pushed ahead on a compass course past the bottom of the heel of Italy, out over the open Adriatic towards the island of Corfu.

We had a head wind against us and it was a dreary flight, but as we neared the mainland of Greece the weather fortunately changed and we passed over the picturesque island of Levkas into the Gulf of Patras under more or less ideal conditions. And then on again to the Gulf of Corinth, over the canal which connects the Gulf with the Aegean Sea, until Athens came into view. On this flight I seemed to derive a great deal of satisfaction from the fact that I had chosen a seaplane for the journey. Although this was about the fifth time that I had flown over this route, all my previous expeditions had been by aeroplane, when I had the constant thought in my mind that I was depending entirely upon my engine, for landing along that rocky coast line would be a difficult feat indeed. But here with a seaplane one felt tempted to alight and rest awhile on these sheltered waters amid such charming scenic surroundings. All the way along from Corfu to Athens every rock seems to play some part in the history and legends of ancient Greece. At last, just before sunset, Piraeus came into view and beyond was Phaleron Bay where we were going to land by the Greek Air Force seaplane base. While circling above this, we had magnificent views away to the north of Athens with the

Acropolis standing out high on its rocky prominence, although on this occasion we troubled little about photographing the scene, as it was necessary for us to get down and refuel before dark.

On nearly every flying expedition in the past I had always considered myself the strong man of the party, but I must confess that at the start of our Australian trip I was done, and on landing at Athens I simply had to hand over the whole show to Elliott, who fortunately appeared to be very fit and cheery. Major Brock, the general manager of the Blackburn Aeroplane Company in Greece, whose factory is at Phaleron, very kindly acted as my host. When I woke on the following morning I realised that I was not in a fit state to proceed on the journey. The doctor advised rest, as I was suffering from exhaustion, for it appeared that I was too run down for even the exhilaration of flying to revive me. And so we stayed a day in Athens while Elliott amused himself by inspecting his machine and engine from end to end and getting a little more familiar with working on the craft while she was afloat, which is a new experience as compared with working on the machine in an aerodrome. After a day's rest I felt much better, and so in the early morning, we attempted to get off over the rollers in a dead calm and make for Leros, but found that owing to our very heavy load this was impossible. On talking the matter over with the Commanding Officer of the flying school, he advised us to wait until about nine o'clock when he said the wind would change its direction, the rollers would temporarily cease, and just as the new wind sprang up would be our chance to get off again. So we waited, and as everything worked to plan, we found ourselves in the air once more heading on a compass course direct for the island of Leros.

Leros belongs to Italy and is a delightful spot in the Aegean Sea some forty-odd miles from the mainland of Asia Minor. Owing to its rugged coast line there is a lovely inland bay whose narrow entrance shelters it against all rough weather. I always think the Aegean Sea in clear weather, with blue sky and brilliant sunshine, is perhaps one of the most beautiful sights in the whole world, especially when seen from aircraft at an altitude of a thousand feet with one's back to the sun. The water is a deep royal blue except in the shallows near the coast line, where are found varying shades of turquoise blue right up to a silver sand beach. We covered the 200-odd miles in just under two hours and then glided into the sheltered waters of the seaplane base at Leros, where we found our Italian friends waiting to receive us.

I think that Leros was the most ideal seaplane base of the whole trip; no violent wind, no tide and no current. Under these conditions we had perfect control, and thus we were able to bring our craft gently up to a little wooden jetty and moor ourselves just as though we were handling a canoe. The water was so clear that we could see easily to the bottom through a depth of twenty feet. In fact Elliott was of the opinion that if he could only keep his eyes open under the water there was sufficient light to swim under the floats and inspect the bottom of them. We quickly took on our extra petrol and then went ashore to have lunch with the Commanding Officer under a rush grass awning. I remember, after the usual aperitif of a glass of vermouth, we had a delightful meal. The inevitable macaroni was followed by a dish of baby octopus – quite a usual thing in this part of the world – which afforded Elliott no end of amusement. One felt one wanted to linger in this delightful spot, but as we had a big job before us we had to get on, and so early in the afternoon we again got into the atmosphere and headed eastwards along the southern coast of Turkey for Alexandretta, our next stop. The last time Elliott and I had visited Alexandretta was when I was piloting Sir Sefton Brancker to Rangoon and back. On that occasion there had been a strong east wind blowing that caused violent down currents off the mountains, so that when we came on the leeward of this range just in front of Alexandretta we had been subjected to a most violent bumping, when both the General's and Elliott's heads had hit the cabin roof more than once. However, this time there was a gentle wind from the west, and we arrived over the bay of this somewhat important port in the north-east corner of the Mediterranean in perfectly calm atmosphere with delightful smooth waters to land on. In my advance instructions I had requested the harbour-master to put down a buoy for us that should be identified by a red flag, but on arriving over Alexandretta I observed that there were several buoys with several red flags so that I hardly knew where to select my mooring. I ultimately chose the southern end of the open bay. My old friend Mr Catoni was out in his new pinnace ready to meet us and I discovered that we should have landed on the other side of the bay. However, this did not matter much and he took us in tow, and thus we sped right over towards the harbour. It was our first experience of being towed through a narrow gateway, and one always imagines on such occasions that wing-tips are going to touch the quay-side, and one has villanous feelings towards any boat which comes within several hundred yards of the aircraft. We arrived right inside the harbour without any mishap and then proceeded to get filled up, and later – after dinner – spent a happy evening recalling memories of the time when we were there two years before.

On the following morning we discovered, as we flew southward and eastward; that we were getting into a more rarified atmosphere, inasmuch as we had greater difficulty in getting off the water, although the conditions were more or less ideal. Our metal propeller was designed to give the maximum performance in the air at cruising speed so that with a very low petrol consumption and with very little load on the engine we were able to cruise with ease at one hundred miles per hour, but somehow we experienced difficulty in getting the seaplane off the water, for great efficiency is needed with a prop in order to get up the primary speed. I have noticed that it takes every bit of power to get up the first thirty-five or forty miles an hour on the water with a seaplane, and here we found our propeller was hardly suitable. It must be known that as the aeroplane gathers speed, and the engine revolutions increase, so does the power of the engine increase. Now we found our propeller was unsuitable for this situation and therefore we decided to change over to the spare propeller that we carried under our machine, which happened to be of a different pitch. We had had two attempts at getting off and, rather than labour our engine unnecessarily over the waters, we just came back to our mooring and set to work to make the necessary change. During this procedure the British Consul circled round our craft on his pinnace. He had on board quite a merry party of visitors, including the French Governor of Alexandretta and many other important people. Evidently he gave instructions to the man at the wheel to cruise round the seaplane, for I noticed that the pinnace, which had just come out from home, was moving continually round us in a complete circle while we changed the propeller. Apparently the Consul was engrossed in conversation, for the pinnace continued to go round and round the seaplane without cessation, until finally I noticed that there were one or two urgent parleys on board with the Consul, after which it began to steer for the harbour. I learnt afterwards that this incessant circling round our craft had been too much for most of the guests on board, inasmuch as many of them were prostrate and were undergoing all the worst agonies of a bad sea voyage. The curious thing was that the Consul seemed oblivious for such a long time to the general state of affairs.

The exact location is unknown, but this admiring group is typical of the many colonial administrators keen to associate with Cobham.

With our propeller changed we discovered we had a much better static thrust and, although our propeller was not quite so efficient in the air, we were able to get of the water with ease. Thus we left Alexandretta, climbed over the mountains and flew over the land eastwards towards the Euphrates, whose course we were going to follow down to Baghdad. We took off from Alexandretta in moderately cool weather and climbed to five thousand feet and then passed over the land for a hundred miles towards the river. On our way we went right over the French military aerodrome where I had landed on several previous occasions, and away to the south we could see the ancient bazaar town of Aleppo. The visibility of this part of the world is generally good and so we saw the Euphrates on the horizon about thirty or forty miles ahead. Then came the rather long and weary flight when we followed its banks for about four hundred miles. Passing over Rakka, the French military outpost, to Deir-ez-Zor and so on down into Iraq, over Ana with its wonderful palm groves and densely cultivated river islands, on towards Ramadi. I have always been impressed by the extraordinary system of irrigation on this part of the river where the river banks are twenty or thirty feet high and there are giant water-wheels which are worked by huge paddles. The force of the current is sufficient to turn the wheels, and on the back of every paddle there is a small pot which enters the water and is lifted high, tipping its contents into a channel which runs away on to the bank above, thus irrigating acres of land which would otherwise be desert.

At Ramadi we left the course of the Euphrates and flew over the sixty odd miles of land towards the River Tigris, and on this flight, as on many others in the late afternoon, we feared not reaching our destination before sunset. I sent a message through to Elliott, because in my cockpit behind the cabin I am all alone and unable to seek the advice of a second person, and so in order to verify my own ideas on the subject I asked him how much more daylight we could reckon on. Elliott, with a very knowing air and a quizzing look at the sun, estimated it at an hour and a half, which was comforting although I knew it to be very optimistic, but it certainly lessened my

worries for the time being regarding our safe arrival before dark.
When Baghdad came into sight we glided down from a moderately
cool atmosphere of five thousand feet towards the river Tigris and
then we realised that we had come right into a temperature vastly
different from the one out of which we had taken off. As we glided
down it was like sinking into an oven, or suddenly diving from the
cool atmosphere of the open sea, into the hottest room of a Turkish
bath. When we were about five hundred feet from the ground I
thought we should be stifled, and later I discovered that it was 110 in
the shade on that day, so no wonder! The fumes of the engine on the
glide seemed to radiate back, if one put one's head over the side of
the cockpit, like flames in one's face. We got down very nicely on the
river, and the wind was blowing conveniently so that we could taxi
ahead into it up stream straight on to our mooring. Elliott was successful in getting hold of the buoy first shot. On all these occasions I
always nipped out of the cockpit as quickly as possible to assist him,
but somehow between us we got muddled up in the ropes and we
suddenly found that we were drifting from our mooring with the
engine stopped. The current was going at about six or eight knots
and we were drifting down stream at an alarming rate; what is more,
we were perilously close to some barges. A launch by this time had
put out to assist us, so that when we found ourselves drifting we
shouted with all our might for them to come to our aid, which they
did. We then threw them a rope which they caught and made fast,
upon which we yelled to them to tow us away from the on-coming
danger. But the native at the wheel, instead of ordering full speed
ahead in the opposite direction to which we were drifting, turned
his bows down stream, spinning us round in a circle and merely
increasing our speed towards the barges which were moored out in
the stream. It seemed certain that we should crash our machine in
the next few seconds, and if vocal effort on our part and all sorts of
language, kind and otherwise, were going to save the catastrophe, we
did our utmost! Evidently in the last second our native friend at the
wheel realised what he was doing, immediately reversed the order of

things and without any regard for the fact that sudden jerks might break ropes and everything, simply turned his pinnace up stream, twisting us again in a complete circle. I shall always have visions of the tail of our craft being whisked round and missing a crash and utter destruction on the barges by a matter of about three inches! However, the danger over we said no more and we were towed up stream, where this time we fixed ourselves firmly to our moorings. It was so hot we could do nothing. We were utterly exhausted and so, after covering up the cockpit and engine, we left the craft in the stream and, went to our quarters for the night.

The following morning I again found myself in a state of collapse. Perhaps it was the sudden heat, and owing to the fact that I was run down I was not in a fit condition to combat the quick change of temperature. However, I managed to get down to the craft.

In this part of the world at this time of year it is only possible to work in the very early hours, before dawn up until about 9 a.m., and so it was essential that if we meant to fly that day we must get off before the great heat of the sun came up. At Baghdad Elliott had many old friends in the Air Force – curiously, several school pals – and they all seemed so keen and interested in the flight that there were at least half a dozen on the seaplane, giving a hand either at filling up or cleaning the plugs, or any job that might assist Elliott. I shall always have distinct memories of sitting on board the gun-boat feeling very sorry for myself, wondering whether I ought to go back to bed or whether I ought to fly on. At last I decided that I should be all right if I could once get in the air, although only a few moments before I had almost made up my mind to take another day's rest. Once in the air we were soon heading down the Tigris towards Bushire in the Persian Gulf, which was our next stop, five hundred miles away.

While we were cruising along I came to the conclusion that one of the great problems of the new age of world aviation would be that of fortifying the human being against the sudden changes of temperature and atmosphere. For example, if we are to fly, as it is anticipated, within the next few years from England to India in a matter of four days, then something must be done to protect the passenger against the sudden change of temperature. For instance, a person might leave London on a cold April morning with a temperature somewhere in the fifties, and after a flight of about three days in moderately cool air at a fair altitude, find himself descending at Basra into a temperature of 110° in the shade or even more. This state of affairs would naturally be a big tax even on a robust constitution, and it might be fatal to a weakling. So here is a problem for our doctors, to find some means of fortifying the human system against such violent changes. Of course for the next few years air routes will be sufficiently slow to make the change of temperature fairly gradual, so that the would-be traveller of today need have no fears in this direction.

After we had crossed over again from the Tigris to the Euphrates and had flown about one hundred and fifty miles I noticed we were getting into a sand-storm region, and a little later we were forced to descend from a comfortable altitude, lower and lower, owing to the thickening sand-storm, until we were flying but a few feet above the river bank, in order to find our way in the blinding dust. From my experience I know that these sand-storms rise to a great altitude, and even if one could fly above them it would be impossible to see the ground beneath and equally impossible to find one's way over a more or less trackless desert. Moreover on a compass course the risk in arriving at one's destination at a high altitude with a thick dust storm raging beneath would be great, for it would be a decided adventure to come down through the blinding dust and find one's exact whereabouts. Therefore rather than take any of these risks we flew low and followed the bank of the river, and as we were in a seaplane fitted with floats we carried on with a feeling of absolute safety, with the knowledge that we could land on the water of the river at a moment's notice should the dust ever become so thick that there was not sufficient visibility for us to carry on. At last this state of affairs occurred and, spotting a native police hut on the bank of the river, I landed on the water nearby, quietly turned our machine and gently beached her on the mud bank. When the propeller stopped, Elliott hopped ashore, taking with him the anchor which he planted deep in the soft earth inland, well away from the bank, remarking as he did so that he thought this was real sound, practical aviation. At the time I was feeling none too energetic and a little worried and depressed at having the original schedule of our flight so changed. Of course we were gathering fresh information and it was all new experience, which was what we were really out for, but even so I could hardly satisfy my anxieties with these observations. Elliott was very cheerful, and soon we had found shelter from the dust and heat in the big mud police hut where the natives had very kindly taken our mosquito nets and rigged them up over rough beds for us to lie on. Then at 9 a.m. in the morning we found ourselves under our nets endeavouring to sleep. Before settling down I had sent a native off on horseback to the nearest telegraph station so that our whereabouts could be notified to the RAF Headquarters at Baghdad. I suppose we must have rested for about an hour when the native police brought us delicious hot tea, Russian style, and after that another fellow brought us a huge melon with ample sugar, much to the delight of Elliott! And so we remained with these kindly folk until about 1.30 or so in the afternoon, when the dust storm lifted a little and I thought we might have another shot at reaching Basra instead of Bushire that day.

All went well for about the first half-hour of our flight, but as we were nearing the beginning of the great swamp area above Basra we ran into another dust storm, and so we continued to fly low. The River Euphrates enters the Hammar Lakes just above the town of Suke Shuyuk when it gradually becomes a mere channel through a vast inundated area. As long as one has a definite horizon or some distinct feature such as a river bank upon which to focus one's gaze it is not a difficult matter to fly in even very bad visibility. It must be remembered that whereas it is a comparatively simple matter for a motor car to go at forty miles an hour along a road with a five or six hundred yard visibility, it is a vastly different thing to pilot an aircraft at one hundred miles an hour with the same visibility and an indefinite horizon. For these reasons I was worried about flying over the open swamp of the lake, because the muddy brown waters merged into the brown dust-laden atmosphere and I felt it would be difficult to distinguish which was water and which was air. When a pilot is enveloped in thick fog and has no horizon whatever, he very quickly loses his equilibrium and cannot make his own level; in fact he loses all sense of where the ground is, or which is top and which is bottom. The same conditions exist in a blinding sand-storm as in a fog, and therefore I felt that if I lost my horizon as a result of the water merging into the sand-storm I might find myself in a very awkward predicament. However, fortunately there were rushes and weeds drifting on the lake which were sufficient for me to distinguish its surface, and this gave me a horizon to work on.

Soon we left the town of Suke Shuyuk behind us, and as we went on I was determined that no matter what direction I might be taking I would follow the somewhat irregular definite coast-line of rush swamp rather than go out on a direct course over the open water. And so, flying at about fifty feet above the reeds, I made a zig-zag course along the somewhat indefinite edge of the lake. I was making for its southern shore where I knew we should meet hard earth and thus have something distinct to see, and although at times I seemed to be flying back on my tracks, I kept on, knowing that eventually we should come out to the hard desert again.

Gradually the swamp area began to give way to the irregular sandy coast-line, and I was just congratulating myself that we should soon be out of our worst difficulties and flying at an altitude of not more than forty feet in order to get the maximum visibility ahead, when suddenly there was a violent explosion which appeared to come from the cabin. Instantly I shouted through the connecting window to Elliott asking him what had happened and if we were on fire, for my first thought was that possibly one of our rocket-pistol cartridges had exploded, and as the rocket burns for many seconds with an intense flame it would certainly set the machine on fire. Elliott shouted back in a very feeble voice that a petrol pipe had burst, but it was difficult to hear him and as I was unable to shut my engine off and glide owing to our very low altitude, I tore a sheet of paper off my writing-pad and handed it through the window to him. Presently a message came back to the effect that the petrol pipe which leads from the reserve tank in the cabin to the supply tank on the top wing had burst a few inches from the point where it was joined to the cabin tank, and that he was hit in the arm very badly and was 'bleeding a pot of blood'. As he handed the message through to me I noticed how terribly pale he looked and I knew that he must be very seriously wounded. Immediately I was confronted with the problem of whether to land and endeavour to render first aid, or whether I had better carry on. I looked beneath me and there was nothing but the dirty brown shallow waters of the great swamp. The heat was terrific and I reflected that even if I did land without the aid of a second man I should most certainly have to drift on the water and run the risk of beaching the machine on a mud bank; and worse still, having rendered what aid I could to Elliott, I should have to start up the machine again single banded – no easy matter when both engine and atmosphere are very hot. Furthermore there would be the difficulty of leaping into my cockpit and taking control of the machine again after the engine had started. Then again I thought, 'Elliott is bleeding and I might be able to stop it,' and yet again I argued that if he were very badly hit he would need a doctor's attention, and to run the risk of trouble through landing in the swamp in a dust-storm, many miles away from any habitation or help, and of being unable to restart – having rendered first aid – seemed wrong. Therefore I made the decision that the only thing to do was to fly on and try to make Basra as quickly as possible, and perhaps this decision was confirmed when a few seconds later I hit up the definite southern desert coast-line of the Hammar Lake, then headed eastwards as hard as I could go to Basra, where I knew there would be every possible assistance and a hospital.

It was 110° in the shade that day and flying low at fifty feet with the throttle wide open did not make for a pleasant trip. The heat was overpowering; gradually my oil temperature rose, and, considering that my engine was air-cooled, it was going to be a severe test. I estimated that we must be nearly a hundred miles from Basra and I was hoping to land on the river there in about forty minutes, so that it might be possible to get medical assistance in under the hour. Our old bus did about a hundred and twenty-five miles an hour full out, and at this speed we hurtled along, skimming over the bank of the lake mile after mile, while all the time I was wishing I could go still faster. It was an enormous relief when the weather began to clear and the dust storm abated, and when within about thirty miles of Basra itself we came out into brilliant sunshine I was able to climb to a more convenient height.

At last the great port of Mesopotamia came into view and I could see the broad river littered with a mass of shipping. The next problem was to know where and how to land. It must be remembered that when one is floating on the water with a seaplane, as long as the engine is running the craft is moving forward and the moment the engine stops, unless there is no current and no wind, the seaplane is drifting either with the wind or with the current.

Now I could see that there would be a strong current running at Basra so I knew that once I had landed I would have to beach the machine on the bank forthwith because, owing to the fact that when taxying there is not enough speed to create sufficient draught to cool the engine, we should very quickly over-heat and run the risk of our engine seizing up. As we passed over the palm groves, to my dismay I discovered that the river had an embankment on each side, or piles, or shipping, or some obstruction or other for miles on either bank and there seemed not a spot with an open mud beach upon which I could run our floats. At last I spied a little mud bank next to a small creek and decided that I must get down on to the water and make that bank. Fortunately there was a clearing of the small craft at that moment on the water beneath and we were able to land quite well, and then I taxied as quickly as possible towards our refuge. It was difficult to steer the machine against the current but, knowing what was at stake, I could not be too particular about damaging our floats, and so at a fair pace I taxied up towards the mud bank, then slowed down and, just as I was about to drift broadside, opened up full throttle and ran the floats high up on the mud. Luckily the mud was soft and we came gently to rest high and dry. So I shut off the engine and got to the cabin as quickly as I possibly could. As soon as I opened the lid I discovered poor Elliott in a terrible state, sitting huddled up on his seat in the corner at the back of the cabin. It was about four o'clock in the afternoon and the heat was terrible; I noticed that he was having great difficulty in breathing. He told me feebly that he was sure he had got a hole in his side and that he was breathing through that hole.

Natives had gathered round, and perhaps the sudden landing of the machine had scared them, for they were most stupid and would render me no aid whatever. However, by sheer force I lugged one up on to the floats and made him stand up and help me lift Elliott down. It was an awful job raising him out of his seat, for I felt that I must inevitably hurt him. At the same time I did not want him to exert himself at all although he was so willing, despite his agonies, to assist in lightening his own weight as I lifted him out. Elliott had always been incredibly methodical with his duties, specially in the matter of engine maintenance, and I shall never forget that while I had him in my arms and was struggling with the assistance of the native to step down from the lower wing, on to the floats, he said to me, 'Turn the oil off' (it was a job that always had to be done immediately the engine stopped), and feebly tried to push down the lever which was close by. As soon as we were off the floats we laid him gently down on the bank and endeavoured to prop his head up with some cushions out of the machine. I had a quick look at his arm and the wound in his side and could see that, apart from temporarily plugging the wounds with cotton wool, I could do nothing. During the flight I had been able to hand him my brandy flask, but after a time be had become too weak to lift it to his lips and so I was now able to give him another drink and then set to work immediately to get help. I wanted a stretcher or bed on which he might be carried, but all the stupid natives did was to run away. Not one would go in search of a doctor; they simply shut their doors in my face when I asked for help. However, at last I got one fellow to go over to the B. O. C. bungalow and warn them that we had a man who must go to hospital, and then I tried again to make some sort of improvised stretcher on which we could lift Elliott. I felt like murdering every fool I came in contact with, but fortunately at this juncture two launches arrived with white men on board who had evidently seen our landing. Very quickly the situation was explained to them, whereupon they rushed to the nearest native hut, walked in, took the first rush-made bed and converted it into a stretcher. On this we lifted Elliott and a few moments later, having left someone to guard the machine, we were speeding down the river towards the B. O. C. bungalow.

Going out of the open air into the bungalow at Basra was like going out of a very hot room into the night air in England, for inside its thick walls the air was cool and we soon had Elliott lying on soft cushions with two electric fans going full out above him. Then came another interminable wait until the doctors arrived, and, although they were tearing in cars full out they had to come a long distance. To me it seemed that they would never come and that they did not realise the gravity of the case, for I suppose by this time I was suffering a certain amount of reaction after a somewhat trying day. A little later Elliott's wounds were temporarily dressed and he was taken away to hospital. I remember Elliott saying that he could not understand how the petrol pipe had burst. In the meantime I went back to the machine and we towed her down the river and up into the backwaters of the Royal Air Force inland water-transport dock and there moored her.

During dinner I endeavoured to explain to the Commanding Officer how it had all occurred, and the engineers present maintained that it was impossible for the petrol pipe to burst, for the simple reason that it was open at both ends and that it was not a pressure pipe, for the petrol was simply lifted by the pump to the top tank. They were convinced that there was no earthly reason why it should burst and even having done so, why it should do so much damage. I went to bed that night with the news that Elliott was doing quite well, but still wondering why it had all happened. The next morning at breakfast the engineer-officer asked me if I had seen any natives about when I was flying over the swamp and I replied that we could see nothing at all for the blinding dust-storm. He then told me that natives were there right enough and that they had shot at us; that it was not the petrol pipe that had caused the damage but a bullet which had entered our machine, pierced the petrol pipe and hit Elliott, and to prove this he took me down to our sea plane and sure enough there was a hole through the cabin side, and the despatch box from the Foreign Office to the Governor-General of Australia which lay against the cabin wall had a hole right through it. Then I planned it all out. The explosion that I had heard had been the firing of the gun, for we were flying so low that the sound of the explosion and the bullet arrived simultaneously. The shot had been fired evidently by an Arab who had pointed his gun at the approaching machine and had fired up at an angle of about 45 degrees. The bullet must have passed between our two floats and just missed the edge of the plane and a couple of flying wires. It then pierced at a slanting angle the wall of the cabin, passed straight through the petrol pipe inside the cabin and then on through Elliott's arm, shattering the bone, on again into his side passing through both lobes of the left lung until it finally buried itself under his right arm-pit.

Headquarters asked me to show them on the map the exact spot where this had occurred, but owing to the prevailing sand-storm it had been impossible to read a map. We therefore decided that the only way in which we could trace the culprit would be to fly back over our tracks, tracing back in an aeroplane the course we had come until I recognised the actual spot where the tragedy had occurred. And so it came about that I journeyed out to the Air Force aerodrome at Shiba with the object of taking off at dawn the next morning in an Air Force machine.

At this stage I was so depressed that I literally had no heart to go on with the flight. I had been to see Elliott, who was in a very weak condition and told me I should have to go on with the job without him, but I assured him I would wait until he got better. The doctors seemed happier now they knew it was a bullet, for they said they could easily extract it and that although Elliott was dangerously ill, there was no reason why he should not pull through. With these thoughts in my mind I spent the late evening with Squadron-Leader Stoddart at Shiba. It was only two short years before that Elliott and I had visited Shiba together on our flight to Rangoon and back, and many of the personnel on the aerodrome were still with the 84th Squadron. We were just about to turn in to bed, in view of our early start on the morrow, when a telephone call came through for me. I found it was a message from the hospital. The connection was very bad and I could hardly distinguish the message, but when I thought I understood what the man at the other end was saying I became nervous and called Stoddart to function for me. So armed with pen and paper Stoddart repeated clearly sentence for sentence – 'Tell Cobham that his engineer Elliott had a sudden relapse and died at 11.15 to-night.'

For a moment I was stunned and could not realise it all; and I made Stoddart ring up again to confirm the news. When I found that it was indeed true I felt that surely now I must give up the flight. I felt I could not go on with it, for this was the culminating point of a depression which had existed almost from the start of the journey. In this state of mind I turned into bed and that is about all I did do, for after interminable wakeful hours the dawn broke at about four o'clock and Stoddart came in to tell me that the machines were being run up and that we were ready to take off in search of the scene of the tragedy. There is rarely much wind in the early morning at this time of year and it is therefore the best period of the day for flying, for as the morning progresses and the sun rises the wind springs up and if it is very strong dust-storms develop such as we had been caught out in on the previous day. There were about four machines in the flight and I went up as passenger with Stoddart, directing him back over the course we had flown the previous day. After just over an hour's flying we came near the place where I had heard the explosion, and in a few minutes I estimated the approximate spot where I thought it had occurred. To make doubly sure we went on beyond until I recognised familiar land-marks we had passed over before we had been fired at, and thus by coming back over our tracks again I was able to locate within a few hundred yards the spot whence the bullet had come. We then flew off to the temporary landing ground at Nasiriya where by previous arrangement we were met by the Political Officer residing in that region. He got aboard one of the other machines and followed us back to the place I had already located, and I fired pistol rockets at the ground to show him the approximate spot. Nearby was an Arab shepherds' encampment, and we flew very low endeavouring to have a look at these people and, as Stoddart said, 'To try and draw the devils' fire.' When I hinted at risk, Stoddart reminded me that ever since 1914, he had never been hit and that his luck was not likely to fail him now! We dived and skimmed over their heads within a few feet, but they were not having any, and not so much as a rifle was raised.

So we reluctantly turned back towards Khamisiyah, a village a few miles away, and there ascertained what tribe was encamped at the place I had identified. With this information we went straight back to the landing ground at Nasiriya and lost no time in getting to the town. The Political Officer was soon informed that the chief of that particular tribe happened that morning to be visiting the town, and within half an hour he had been found and detained in the local gaol pending investigations. From then onwards the investigations progressed which led to the ultimate identification and confession of the Arab who had committed the crime. But all this occurred some weeks afterwards, of course.

I continued to be so depressed that I felt it was hardly worthwhile carrying on with the flight. Elliott had been with me so long and on so many expeditions, and to my mind his death was a severe loss to British aviation. The success of aviation has been built up on its reliability, and the greater proportion of that reliability depends upon the successful maintenance of aircraft by the engineers, and I shall always think of Elliott as one of the finest examples of what an aircraft engineer should be. He was systematic, could always organise his work, was absolutely reliable, and altogether typical of that new race of engineers that has developed with the advance of flying.

I think it must have been the kind telegrams of encouragement from England that showed me clearly what I ought to do. My wife urged me to continue the flight. Then came cables of sympathy from Sir Samuel Hoare, Sir Sefton Brancker, Sir Charles Wakefield and Mr Siddeley, all expressing the hope that I would carry on, so the next job was to find someone to take the place of poor Elliott. It was first suggested that a new man should come out from England, but owing to the missing of connections it appeared that nobody could reach me for about three weeks, which seemed a terrible waste of time. The Siddeley-Jaguar engine, although extensively used by the Air Force of the British Isles, had never been in service in Mesopotamia, and so there was great difficulty in finding anyone

RAF pall-bearers carry Arthur Elliott to his resting place in Basra Cemetery.

Arthur Elliott's headstone in Basra's military cemetery. Unfortunately the wording is inaccurate; Sir Alan's name is spelled incorrectly and the dates quoted for flying from London to Australia actually cover the period for both the outbound and return journeys.

in the Air Force who knew much about this motor. However, the
Air Force very kindly offered to lend me any mechanic that I might
find in Mesopotamia who was capable of helping me to continue
my flight and willing to go. After a brief search one by the name of
Sergeant Ward was discovered who had a slight knowledge of the
Jaguar engine in theory, although no actual running experience. He
was heartily recommended by everyone as a sound engineer and a
very hard worker, and after meeting Ward I decided that he was my
man if he cared to go. The Commander-in-Chief readily granted
him permission and leave, so that within a few days and after we had
given the machine a quick overhaul we said goodbye to Basra and
all its unhappy associations, heading southward on the next jump of
our long flight. Everyone at Basra had done all they could to help
us and render us every possible assistance, but even so I am afraid
that during the whole of my stay there I must have been very poor
company and not so appreciative as I might have been under different circumstances.

CHAPTER II

BASRA TO RANGOON

Ward, like myself, was a Cockney, with a big sense of humour, and therefore I felt from the start that we should get on well together. Soon after dawn on 14 July we took off from the river at Basra and headed for Bushire. Just after sunrise the air is moderately cool at ground level, and it was a weird experience to take off in this comfortable atmosphere and, as we climbed, to enter a hot belt of air that intensified as we climbed higher. I should say we met this belt at about five hundred feet and did not get out of it until we were at least 2,500 feet up. This is evidently caused by the hot air of the previous day rising during the night.

We were making for the head of the Persian Gulf and were passing over some desolate, uninhabited, flat swamp areas, when I had the one and only uncomfortable moment with my engine during the whole flight. For some unknown reason the motor started to slow down and although I opened the throttle it did not instantly rectify the trouble; I was beginning to get alarmed and so immediately headed for the river. There was no spluttering of the engine; no instrument on the dash-board suggested any failure such as low pressure or high temperature; petrol taps were fully turned on, and yet one could hear that the revolutions of the engine were dying down and the revolution indicator showed a fall of about two hundred revolutions. It was a very alarming experience. But suddenly the revolutions rose again and from that day to this I have never discovered what happened or why it happened, and I can only surmise that there might have been some temporary obstruction in the petrol supply which might have caused this unusual incident. I mention it because on our whole flight of twenty-eight thousand miles the Jaguar engine never gave us a moment's anxiety apart from this. During all those long, weary hours in the cockpit, the motor simply purred and purred without a single miss or suggestion of a falter.

This somewhat unpleasant experience over, I again headed towards the sea-coast, when I happened to notice that the petrol in the top tank was getting low. Now it was so arranged that we carried fifty-five gallons of petrol in the top tank which fed the carburetters by gravity feed, and one hundred gallons in a large tank inside the cabin. The top tank had to be kept supplied by pumping petrol from the tank in the cabin up to it. In order to save weight and add to reliability we dispensed with the idea of a wind-vane automatic petrol pump, and had a straight-forward simple hand-pump by which method the mechanic in the cabin could easily feed the top tank at the instructions of the pilot, because the pilot had a view of the petrol gauge in the top tank. Therefore when I noticed that the top tank was just under half full I handed a message through the window to Ward telling him to start pumping up, whereupon Ward set to, full of energy, pumping away. After about ten minutes I happened to notice that there was no progress whatever so I yelled through to Ward that something must have gone wrong. Ward seemed perplexed and pumped the harder, but after five more minutes of strenuous work I became concerned because the petrol was getting perilously low and I doubted if we could reach Bushire on the remaining fuel in the tank. Anyway I meant to go as far as I could and I again yelled through to Ward to do his utmost. Ward by this time was getting exhausted, his head was going with terrific jerks and I felt that if the pump were not already broken it very soon must be. Things were looking desperate when I suddenly remembered that there was a petrol cock at the bottom of the pump and it occurred to me that this might have been turned off during our stay at Basra. So I signalled Ward to this effect and sure enough that was the trouble. As soon as this little matter was rectified I saw to my relief that the petrol was rising in the gauge at the top of the tank and our worries were over. Of course we always speak lightly of our little difficulties afterwards, but at the time such matters are rather disturbing.

As we neared Bushire we ran through a very heavy ground mist and we finished up the first stage of our new start by creeping into Bushire harbour with a visibility of about five hundred yards. Luckily I had been there before, otherwise it would have been far more difficult. When we landed we found everybody much concerned about us owing to the mist, because it appeared that a pinnace which that morning had gone out to a big steamer anchored about a mile out to sea had lost its way.

The mist was very thick indeed, but happily we found that owing to it the air was about ten degrees cooler, which was a great relief after the temperature of Basra. As Ward was new to his job I decided that we would go no further that day, but instead would stay the night at Bushire and thus give him a chance to get down to the general organisation of both machine and engine. The proper maintenance of engine or craft is simply a system of performing at regular periods a schedule of inspections. For instance, after every landing we always inspected the oil-filter, which should give us any indication of internal trouble with the engine and also ensure that through grit or foreign matter our oil pressure should not fail. Again, after every flight petrol filters were always cleaned; and at the end of the day valve-springs and valve-stems were inspected and the engine generally looked over. After so many hours' flying the clearances on the tappets had to be checked, and in a like manner magnetos and every other part of the plane were overhauled. Besides this, of course, the controls of the aeroplane were periodically inspected, so that by going through the schedule according to plan any trouble that might be developing would be observed by the engineer in good time. By these methods we have developed a system of maintenance of aircraft that has brought British aviation up to its present state of reliability.

We had a pleasant flight down the Persian Gulf, passing along this very rocky coast-line with its wonderful, weird rock-formations which extend for miles with precise regularity, especially at one spot where layers of strata seem to overlap one another so that the mountain appears like a gigantic tiled roof. Just before arriving at Bandar Abbas we came upon some wonderful oxide formations. I had seen these before on my flight to Rangoon and had been struck by their vivid colouring. There are mountains and hills of varying hues, such as a sugar-loaf formation towering up several hundred feet, of a brilliant turquoise blue; then close by a similar mass of perfect jade green; and in the background a mountain of indigo blue beside a range of bright yellow hills, while in the foreground rise mounds of bright red rock. In between these amazing masses of colour are streaks of silver formed by the silver sand of ancient dried up river-beds. Away to the south in a deep blue sea we saw the island of Hormez, of a similar oxide formation, and it was there that the Portuguese had mines in centuries gone by. It is my great hope that one of these days we shall be able to photograph these wonderful sights with colour photography.

When we arrived at Bandar Abbas we discovered that a very big sea was running and, what was worse, the wind was not blowing in exactly the same direction as the breakers were running. Now, as everybody probably knows, an aeroplane always lands head into the wind, so that if the landing speed of the aeroplane is forty miles an hour and it lands against a wind blowing twenty miles an hour, then the actual speed over the earth is only twenty miles an hour; and, conversely, if one lands with the wind, the machine would touch ground at sixty miles an hour. Now a seaplane must land at right-angles to the breakers so that it rides over the top of them, otherwise one float would be right down in the hollow and possibly the other would be right up on the crest of the wave, as the sea is on the move all the time and the aircraft also. This state of affairs might be very serious, as the extended wing-tips when put over at this violent angle so near the water might easily be dipped under a breaker with disastrous results. Under these conditions my feelings may be imagined when I discovered that the wind was blowing at an angle of 45 degrees to the roll of the breakers. However, as the sea was running so high I decided to land slightly across the wind, but directly head on to the wave courses, and in this manner we got down safely. The moment we came to rest on the water we were pitched and tossed about in a violent manner, but luckily a launch was waiting to take us to our moorings and without any great difficulty we were soon tied up.

The heat at Bandar Abbas was even greater than at Basra, and evidently exposure in the open cockpit for three or four hours was beginning to tell on me a little; so, leaving Ward on the craft, I decided to go ashore immediately and at the same time ascertain the possibility of beaching the machine, as the sea was so rough that the continual buffeting that the craft was getting would hardly do her any good. By the time I got ashore I was fairly well exhausted, but I found Dr Mackay – one of those brave men carrying on in the unpleasant places of the earth – waiting under an awning with cold drinks, in fact iced drinks, for a ship had just come in that day bringing a supply of ice and the Doctor very sportingly shared it with us. I found that lumps of ice applied to the back of the neck had a fine reviving effect, and after a few more drinks I was ready to consider the next move. We decided then and there to beach the machine, and so went out again and towed our bus in, and as the tide was going out she was left high and dry on the sand. Later on a new difficulty presented itself, because the sea became rougher, and when next the tide came in we discovered that the oncoming breakers would rush under the machine, lift the floats and drop her down again on the beach. This of course would spell disaster; despite the fact that our floats were metal, such a bumping of them on a sandy bottom would soon put holes in them, and this would mean the ruination of the flight. So the only thing to be done was to wait until the tide came in, hold the machine down firmly until there was sufficient water to launch her again and then hold her in position while she floated in a safe depth until such time as the tide went down again, when we would rebeach the machine. Unfortunately high tide was about 2 p.m. and 2 a.m., so that owing to the fact that the sea was so rough that we were unable to get off again that day, it meant that we had to get up at one o'clock in the morning to refloat the seaplane, stand waist deep in the warm, sticky salt water for an hour and a half or two hours, and then rebeach the machine.

On the second day it blew hard, from sunrise until dusk, and a hundred yards from the water's edge the breakers were anything up to six or eight feet high, so that it was impossible to contemplate taking off with a seaplane. The rollers were thirty and forty feet apart and therefore, as our floats were only twenty-odd feet long, it was impossible to ride over them. Had we endeavoured to open up our engine under these conditions we should simply have mounted the first roller and fallen down and plunged underneath the next one, which might have swamped us completely. In order to forecast the weather conditions we got an interpreter to talk with the local fishermen and it seemed probable that the wind might drop as nightfall came on and that in all probability the sea would be moderately calm at dawn on the following morning. So with this prospect we decided that when the tide came up at 2 a.m. we would refloat the machine and tow her out to a mooring and there leave her at anchor during the night, ready for an early start at sunrise. My previous visit to Bandar Abbas had been at a different season of the year when the climate, though warm, had been clear and delightful. But during the summer months, such as we were passing through, Bandar Abbas is not a pleasing place.

The atmosphere was hazy, dull and heavily laden with dust so that the visibility was only a fraction of what it is in normal times, and the temperature was nearly 100 in the shade. Although this was not exceedingly hot, it was a wet, sticky heat and everything one touched was clammy and gritty with the perpetual dust and fine sand that one seemed to inhale continually. Under these conditions the inevitable physical depression set in and then in the weary delay of our progress I think we both became mentally depressed. We perspired freely all day and all night, and that sensation on waking to find one's sheet and mattress soaked with one's own perspiration will always be one of the unpleasant recollections of my flight to Australia.

According to instructions a native bearer wakened me at 1 a.m. out of a semi-stupor (for it could hardly be called sleep) and somehow I managed to drag myself off the bed, pull on a couple of garments and slip my feet into some shoes in readiness to go down to the machine. I was so exhausted that it took all my will-power and concentration to prevent myself from falling back on the bed and dozing off again. While we sat on the verandah for a few minutes drinking a cup of tea by the light of a smoky oil lamp, for it was pitch dark, it was only with the greatest difficulty, when Sergeant Ward and our host, the bank manager, said that all was ready, that I could drag myself out of the chair. It was a pitch-black night – no stars, no moon. We followed our guide, equipped with one dirty oil lamp with glass half smoked over, along a winding track between the sand-dunes towards the beach. When we arrived we found a party of natives on the beach waiting for us as arranged, and we estimated that in ten minutes the tide would be sufficiently high to allow us to refloat the craft and tow her out to the mooring. With about six men in the boat we soon had the machine floating and were successfully pulled out into the open sea. Gradually our eyes became sufficiently accustomed to the darkness to see that we were pulling out more or less at right angles to the beach. Now there is plenty of open sea at Bandar Abbas; no rocks and no obstructions, and with the exception of a small motor-launch called the 'Felix Jones' which belonged to the British Consul and which must have been three or four hundred yards from our mooring, there was no other craft on the water. Presently, away on the starboard I could see the dim shape of the 'Felix Jones' and warned the boatmen about it. Owing to a slip in the arrangements there was no interpreter aboard and as the natives did not understand my language (and I am sure nobody understood theirs) my shoutings and gesticulations appeared to have no effect on the crew of the rowing boat and so we drew nearer and nearer to the motor launch. I gradually realised that they were unable to find the moon in the dark and they intended to tie the seaplane up to the 'Felix Jones' and leave it moored out in this fashion. Although this was not exactly ideal I reflected that both launch and seaplane would swing more or less into the wind and I thought she would be reasonably safe till morning, as the sea was not very rough now. There was a strong current running at the time making it desirable to approach the launch against the current, but instead the fools in charge towed us round the bows of the launch so that we naturally drifted down on to it.

When I look back on this incident it always strikes me how stupid the whole affair was, because there was a vast expanse of sea with just one obstruction in it, which they seemed unable to miss. The moment they towed us round the front of the launch they ceased rowing and naturally, as they were down current, the seaplane drifted on to the boat and the whole lot drifted to the launch together, but so badly did they manage affairs that whereas they drifted on to the port side of the launch the seaplane, which was being towed on a good length of rope, was allowed to drift on to the starboard side And then came the crash. When our precious seaplane, in which we had flown all the way from England, and in which we still hoped to fly to Australia and back, collided with the rails of the launch and I could hear the cracking and crunching of timbers, of wings breaking, and, after a moment's pause while the waves bore her away a bit, and then back again, more cracking and more splitting of spars and ribs, I was in despair. She drifted on at such an angle that the starboard wing-tip and the starboard tail-tip collided with the launch; when I had seen disaster coming I had managed to leap from the boat to the launch and just get to the tail in time, but despite all my strength I could not hold off the entire weight of the seaplane, although I think I lessened the force of the blow with which the tail kept bumping the launch rails. But there was no one to hold off the wing-tip in the same way, and so I shouted to Ward to come aboard and help. Now an unfortunate coincidence which nearly caused tragedy was the fact that our host the bank manager's name was Ward, as well as that of my engineer. Sergeant Ward had gone out on the floats of the seaplane and so was unable to get to the wing-tip and render assistance, and when I had yelled for help I had meant our host in the rowing boat to get a native to come and hold the wing-tip. But still no one got out of the boat, our host still thinking I was addressing my remarks to Sergeant Ward! I yelled to the natives, but they simply sat there like idiots, content to watch the whole machine sink. I was almost in tears, because here was the embodiment of all my hopes and ambitions being wrecked and ruined before my very eyes, while I was powerless to prevent it.

I called to them to help; I cursed them in every language known, but all to no avail. There was a lull in the waves for a moment and I was just able to leave the tail, rush to the boat edge and use my foot with all the force I could muster round the heads and bodies of the crew in the boat. I dragged them on to the launch and thus I got two on the tail-tip and two more on the wing-tip and in this position we held her and got breathing space. Of course by this time the damage was serious and it was useless to leave her there with the idea of taking off in the morning, for I knew she would have to be taken ashore again to be repaired if possible the next day.

Now the native has a very stupid temperament. They all knew they had failed dismally in this job, and they knew that if they had to tow her back everyone would know they had failed; therefore I found them very reluctant to obey my orders to get us ashore again – in fact it was only by dint of physical effort and threats of death that I managed to persuade these poor, half-witted, cross-bred, nondescript coolies of the Persian Gulf. Eventually we reached the beach again and pulled our floats up on to the hard sand. It was too dark to inspect the machine then and, as I knew she would be safe because it was not high tide until midday, we struggled back to the bungalow again in a state of utter exhaustion and dejection. For my part I flung myself on the bed, not caring what happened, but knowing that we had a further delay now, and tried to cheer myself with the fact that we were not completely wrecked.

The next morning on inspecting the wing-tips and tail we discovered that the damage was not nearly so bad as we expected, and we were able with a few minor repairs to have the machine ready for flight by about midday. By this time the sea was rough again but as the breakers were quite moderate, at least as far as I could see, and as the fishermen assured me that there were no big breakers out at sea, I decided to risk starting, because all the breakers I could get a view of from the beach were not big enough to do us serious harm; so we warmed our engine up all ready to take off. We were very heavily laden and I estimated that we should require a reasonable run to get off, but provided the breakers beyond my view from the beach were not greater than I could see, we should be all right and we just opened out again to gather up speed. It was no easy matter to handle the seaplane, because each wave-crest seemed to hit the floats with a particularly heavy thud and I had to be most careful that the floats did not miss a crest and dive down under a wave, for this would mean a bank of water flooding over the floats and deluging the propeller and engine, which of course would not be at all good for either. We were just beginning to work up speed and had got up well on to the first step of our floats when we came to more or less open sea, and here to my horror I discovered giant breakers which I knew were far too big for us.

However, as we had gathered up a fair amount of speed there was a possibility that I might be able to ride the crests of the waves, and so I carried on for a second longer. But I quickly discovered this was impossible and then came the terrible period when I had to throttle down amid this awful pitching sea, praying that I should not be swamped and should get nothing broken. As the engine slowed down, so we plunged deeper into the waves with more sickening thuds, and I was only too thankful when at last we stopped. Then we had a new difficulty because it was vital to keep our machine head on to the wind, otherwise, if she got broadside on owing to the violent pitching and tossing, our wing-tips would be thrust under the waves and the wings broken. It was difficult to keep the engine running, for a deluge of water kept breaking over the lower cylinders and of course such conditions were of no use to the propeller, which ran the risk of being broken any moment by the waves. We had unfortunately lost our sea-anchor, but even if we had had it Ward would have found it almost impossible to get out on to the floats, as he might easily have been washed overboard, so violently were we being hurled up and down. Luckily we were drifted backwards head on to the breakers and thus we came back into water sheltered enough for natives to wade and swim out to us. But here again their stupidity nearly wrecked us, for instead of man-handling our machine back the way we were drifting, namely head on to the breakers, they started to turn her so that they could bring her in head on to the beach, disregarding the fact that in the process of turning we should have to get broadside to the waves and run the risk of getting our wings under the water and broken as the machine heeled over at a perilous angle in the act of riding a big breaker. Here again Ward found that the only way to save the machine was to use his toe in tender spots of his fellow-creatures who had swum out to help and thus, by dint of much shouting and here and there the further application of the said toe, we were man-handled backwards, keeping our head on to the breakers until we were finally beached and were safe once more. We found that the undercarriage strut had been broken, which necessitated a further delay for repairs. Ward was not disheartened, but set to work immediately to take the damaged strut off. We then went up to the Consulate to see what materials we could find to patch the machine up.

About six years before, some Handley-Page spare parts had been put down in the Persian Gulf for a flight which was conducted by Sir Geoffrey Salmond along the Persian Gulf to India. Among the spare parts was a Handley-Page centre-section strut which we persuaded the clerk-in-charge to let us have, although he was very reluctant to do so as he maintained it ought to be kept for a Handley-Page machine – despite the fact that that particular type was obsolete many years since. After stripping the fairing off the strut we discovered a round tube inside, and Ward worked like a Trojan, stripped to the waist and with about four natives round him. He proved an excellent blacksmith because we found that when we hammered the round tube into an oval shape it fitted inside the oval tube of our under carriage strut with absolute precision to the thousandth part of an inch. So we refitted our strut, and the repair held good for the rest of the journey to Australia and back again to England.

Two days later we finally got away from Bandar Abbas and headed down the Persian Gulf to Chahbar. We arrived about midday, our intention being to fill up and push on to Karachi. There were some nasty rollers at the time and we had just completed filling up when Ward stepped on a float that wasn't there and disappeared into the sea. I was rather perturbed about this, but a few seconds later I was helping to pull him up over the floats little the worse for his severe ducking. It was one of the fears of my life during this flight that someone would fall off the floats and be unable to regain hold of them on account of the strong under-current that would drag him under the water, with the possibility of being exhausted before help were available. So I was always warning Ward about falling in and furthermore about dropping things in. One of the important things an engineer must remember when working on a seaplane in the open sea is that, unless he has a sheet underneath the engine, whatever he drops he loses, and if he happens to let slip through his fingers some vital part of the engine it might be a severe handicap to the expedition. We only just managed to get off from Chahbar over the rollers and then headed eastwards down the coast towards Karachi. It was a misty day but we had a fairly good flight and at last when Karachi came into view we could see two launches out in the spacious harbour waiting to meet us.

Now at Karachi there is a large aircraft depot which supplies the whole of India with its new machines and necessary spares, and naturally they were going to take an interest in us and render all possible assistance. It also happened that the Commanding Officer of the Air Force depot was an old seaplane pilot and was naturally looked upon as an authority on the subject of my landing. He therefore gave his skilled advice regarding all the arrangements that were made for our arrival, although, as we were landing in the harbour, the Port Officer was the man responsible for our reception. Among other things, the CO warned everyone not to be annoyed if I were a little vexatious on landing. He explained that, being an old seaplane pilot himself, he knew the anxieties that would be mine. He reminded them how I had brought this seaplane all the way from England and hoped to take it all the way to Australia and possibly back again, and that I was nursing it like a baby; and that like an anxious mother with her child I should probably imagine that everyone was out to destroy us. Therefore he cautioned all boats not to come anywhere near us on landing lest I let forth unpleasing language – a quite common and excusable thing for a seaplane pilot to do when landing his craft. He told them they must bear with me until I was ashore, for then I should be quite human again. Well, we made quite a good landing on the water and I taxied a little way until I saw the launch, and then rather than get my engine too hot (for an air-cooled engine is only kept so by its speed through the air) I shut it off and waited for the launch to come and take us in tow. Ward was standing on the end of one float and I on the other, each of us ready to catch the heaving line when thrown to us, whereupon we would attach our main mooring rope and they would haul in and take us in tow. The launch crept forwards and an Air Force fellow in his shirt was standing up in the bows of the boat with heaving line ready to throw to us. His first effort missed us hopelessly and so he had to gather his rope in again and prepare to throw once more. This very often happens, and as we had plenty of room there was no need to worry. However, he took a long time to recoil the rope and we were drifting in the direction of some boats. Again this man attempted to heave the line, but this time caught it on a hook in his own boat. This meant re-coiling the rope once more. Then a third time be heaved, but somehow got the rope caught round his own neck and there was a glorious muddle up, during which he tried to re-coil the rope while I shouted to him to heave as we were drifting towards the barges. My shouts seemed unavailing for there was no sign of the rope coming over, so I yelled still louder, adding one or two adjectives regarding the rope, hoping that they would act as a stimulant as the barges were getting nearer and nearer every moment. But still the rope was going through the slow process of being re-coiled and muddled up, and knotted up, and entangled – and I was becoming desperate. I had already had five days' worry and this day we had just flown between seven and eight hundred miles, so that I was in no mood to be lenient with anyone. Thus it came about that I began to shout without restraint and apply adjectives regarding both the rope and the wielder of it, until at last with a final mighty effort our friend heaved the rope, which we managed to grab as it floated in the water and were taken in tow just in time. I noticed that all the Port Authorities aboard the launch were grinning and tittering and I could see there was some huge joke afoot. I was not long in discovering what it was, for it transpired that our friend the heaver of the rope was none other than the Commanding Officer of the Air Force depot himself!

I was glad we were through the Persian Gulf because I have come to the conclusion that the open sea from Karachi to Bushire in most cases is very unfavourable for a seaplane or a flying boat of any type. There seem to be permanent rollers, especially in the Gulf of Oman, although there were many wonderful sheltered bays that would make excellent hydroplane bases. Unfortunately Bandar Abbas and Chahbar, although they had good aerodromes, were useless as sea-plane bases, and therefore I decided that on the return journey I would go to a place called Laft which is in the sheltered Clarence Strait about forty miles west of Bandar Abbas.

It was a great relief to arrive at Karachi, for we were back in civilisation once more with communication, help, and every facility, and I shall never forget that happy feeling as I lolled back in my host's car as be drove me from the quay-side to his bungalow, where hot baths and clean changes awaited us. Although very tired I felt distinctly refreshed and acquired a completely new outlook on the prospects of my job.

At Karachi, too, we were greatly assisted by the Air Force who helped to give our machine a quick overhaul. Repairs were made to the damage done at Bandar Abbas, our floats were thoroughly inspected, and repainted, and then on the second day after our arrival we took off and headed north-eastwards for Bahawalpur. Our course at the start lay due east over the desert towards the River Indus. Fortunately we had a following wind, but against this we had the unpleasant experience of having to fly through a dust storm. After about 80 miles we came to the Indus and then followed its course northwards, as Bahawalpur is situated on one of its tributaries over four hundred miles further up. The sand storm got worse as we progressed and we were forced to fly low along the river, following its bank which proved extremely difficult because it was very much in flood. Owing to the sand-storm I could not get to any great height, and furthermore the visibility was so poor that owing to the innumerable creeks and backwaters I could never definitely ascertain my exact position, or whether I was following up the correct tributary on which Bahawalpur was situated. However, at the point where I made my final turn for Bahawalpur the Indus made a direct curve northward, whereas my course lay due east, and so by checking this up with the compass I had a good idea of where I was going. It was a long and weary flight and for the last hour I was very worried because I had estimated arriving much sooner. When therefore at the allotted time Bahawalpur did not come into view on the horizon I began to calculate and check up on my map to find if we had taken the wrong course.

This doubt remained until at last I saw the great railway bridge ahead just above Bahawalpur and knew that our troubles so far were over. The heat had been terrific and although I wore coloured glasses the continual glare of the waters of the Indus had affected me, so after landing and mooring up I felt in a very distressed and gasping condition. There was an old launch towed alongside where preparations had been made for our arrival, and as soon as I got aboard they quickly revived me with slabs of ice on my head and the back of my neck. I had no idea that this treatment could have such a miraculous effect, for I was O.K. in five minutes.

At Bahawalpur the temperature was 110 in the shade, but much drier than it had been down the Gulf and therefore not quite so hard to bear. After a very pleasant evening, during which I had been able to get my dispatches and correspondence up to date, we were ready again on the following morning to push on another four hundred miles by a land route towards Delhi, when we should jump from the waters of the Indus over to the Jumna.

Landing and taking off on rivers is no easy matter, especially if there is a strong current running. At Bahawalpur it was not difficult, as it was possible for natives to stand in the water and hold our machine in position while we ran the engine up and made preparations to start. The conditions for the take off were more or less ideal because head into the wind meant taking off down current, which all tended to make a speedy get-off. All I had to beware of were some sand-banks a little way down the river, and I had to make sure of being in the air before we reached this spot. I had arranged that the moment I put my hand above my head all the natives should leave go of the floats and I should open out my engine and take off straight away. And so with everything in readiness and Ward in the cabin with lid bolted down, I put my hand high above my head, and seeing all the natives jump away, opened out the engine and began to get up speed. The art of taking-off with a sea plane is first to prevent the floats from dipping into the water, for there is a tendency to do this immediately on opening up the engine unless one pulls the control lever well back so that the elevators lift the nose of the machine at the start; next, as a little speed is gathered, comes the process of pushing the control lever right forward in an endeavour to get the tail up, because owing to the increasing speed there is no fear at this point of the floats dipping into the water, until such time as the tail rises up and the machine gets on to the step underneath the floats, when it quickly gathers greater speed. The control lever is then eased back a little and the wings begin to lift her off the water.

I had about reached this stage and was just going to ease the machine off the water when I happened to notice some poor wretched native hanging on to the floats. It was only by sheer luck that I looked that way, otherwise I might have found myself in the air with a native dangling from my floats prior to making a very unpleasant plunge to the water beneath. The moment I noticed him I throttled down again and shouted to Ward to get out of the cabin and make the fellow get off, because the river was too narrow for me to turn in, and I did not want to stop my engine, and worse still we were getting near the sandbanks ahead. The native took no notice of our shouts so I told Ward to get him off at all costs, whereupon we very cruelly pushed the poor fellow into the water by treading on his hands until he had to leave go. I do not think I could have been capable of such an act had we not been tuned up to the emergency of the moment. Immediately he left go and disappeared under the water, I straightway opened out and before Ward was properly in the cabin again we had gathered speed once more and were taking off into the atmosphere. It was at this point that I realised what we had done, and I looked round, trusting that the fellow was safe, for the natives are all wonderful swimmers. Our fears were allayed when we saw a party of natives come to his rescue and drag him out, for I heard on my return flight that curiously enough this poor creature could not swim and had got nervous at the last moment and dared not let go of the floats.

We left Bahawalpur in a dust-laden atmosphere, and rather than take the winding course of the river, or on the other hand push out into this bad visibility on a compass course, I followed the railway, which is more or less direct. Thus we skimmed along at about one hundred feet for a couple of hundred miles until we came to the ancient city of Bhatinda, where the visibility began to be clear and we got into comparatively brilliant sunshine and so continued south-eastward until we came to Delhi. The Burma Oil Company had made full arrangements for our fuel supplies and landing facilities across India and Burma to Rangoon, and without their help I am afraid our passage would have been very difficult. We landed on the Jumna at Delhi and luckily got into our moorings first shot. Getting up to one's moorings single-handed without the aid of a launch, specially when there is either a strong wind blowing or a strong current running, is a very difficult business with a seaplane, because the machine has to be taxied over the water to the mooring. Very often owing to the wind and current, it was a most difficult procedure to keep control over the direction of the machine so that I could bring the starboard floats up within a foot or so of the mooring buoy to enable Ward, standing on the float with a boat hook, to catch hold of the buoy and make fast.

At Delhi we landed very well. Fortunately a strong wind was blowing down the river, so that we had to land up-wind and up-current, which was ideal from a landing point of view; and thus we were able, owing to the wind and current, to taxi very slowly up to the mooring where we easily made fast. We were not long in re-fuelling and were ready to take off again when we discovered that we could not start the engine up. Poor Ward turned and turned the crank-handle while I turned the self-starter magneto, all to no purpose, for after spluttering a few turns the propeller would stop. Now this was the first time in all my experience of the Siddeley-Jaguar engine that she had failed to start up, so Ward being exhausted and the hour getting too late for us to reach our destination before dark, I considered it best to stay at Delhi to give Ward time to inspect his engine. This naturally meant staying the night. The next morning, despite the fact that Ward had thoroughly inspected the ignition magnetos and been well over the whole machine, we still had the same difficulty. I was convinced that the cause of the trouble lay in the petrol supply, but on inspection this appeared to be perfect. I then remembered that it was our custom to wedge a large piece of rag in the air-intake pipe to prevent sand and such foreign bodies getting into the carburettor. Two of these wads in the intake pipes had been sucked right down, and when they were removed our engine started up first shot.

Now when the engine starts is the time to cut adrift, but we discovered that we could not get head up-stream and were afraid to cast adrift because the wind, which was blowing across the river, blew our tail round and pointed our nose into the bank.

It must be remembered that a seaplane on the water is like a weather-cock and is automatically kept head into the wind by its keel surface. At the same time the current at this point of the river was running at about ten knots and washing into the bank so that we found it impossible to get away from the bank, and therefore could not run the risk of opening up our engine and getting away from our moorings. We were being held in the creek in position by ropes from either bank and the work of organising these gangs of natives was exciting. Ward was a wonderful fellow in such emergencies. His energy was untiring and he seemed to live in a bathing costume, and was everywhere at the same moment. Suddenly one rope broke and we found ourselves drifting across the creek on to a stone embankment. Had it not been for the presence of mind of Ward, who leapt into the water just in time to hold the drifting machine off, we should have met with disaster. Again ropes were fixed and now I decided that I must go once more into the open river and that natives would have to hold me in position facing up by means of long ropes, and that they would have to let these ropes out quickly as I opened up my throttle, so that I could immediately get up speed enough for my controls to act, owing to our forward pace, above the force of the wind and the current. The only drawback to such a procedure was that it was impossible for Ward to cut us free from the ropes and leap into the cabin with the engine running full out. This business would take at least a few seconds and, unless I was able to open out full blast the moment the ropes were cut, I should find myself again in the bank and unable to get up sufficient speed to turn up stream before we collided. A very plucky native sergeant-major came forward at this juncture and volunteered to solve the difficulty. It would be all right for Ward to get into the cabin, he said, for he would go out on to the floats and as I opened up and the natives let the ropes out and the machine gained speed, the moment I was going fast enough to have complete control I was to raise my hand; he would then cut the ropes and jump off into the water and swim ashore. It must be remembered we were held by ropes hundreds of yards long on either side and so there was sufficient rope to be let out to get up speed, and as I started I opened out and very quickly got control and headed the machine away from the bank. Then when I was doing thirty miles an hour I raised my arm, and instantly the plucky sergeant-major set to work and cut the ropes. As the last rope was severed we must have been doing forty miles an hour, when he slipped quietly off the floats into the water and disappeared out of sight. Then came the terrible take-off in which we had to go up the river, crossing against the current and wind. I shall be eternally grateful to our good friend the native sergeant-major for his timely help; as we flew back over the river I was glad to see he had got safely ashore and was waving us farewell.

Our flight from Delhi to Allahabad was uneventful, and I had time to notice the difference in the countryside as compared with my previous visit, which had been in the winter time two years before. Everywhere natives were at work in the fields benefitting by the start of the monsoon, and already the ground was green with the crops coming up. We left the River Jumna and crossed over the land for a distance of a hundred miles to the Ganges, whose course we followed until it converged with the Jumna again before reaching Allahabad.

When we arrived at Allahabad I found they had marked my landing places out in the wide flood waters of the Jumna with six huge buoys, each one being quite big enough and strong enough to hold a battleship, let alone a seaplane. They were like immense floating iron tanks that towered about six feet out of the water and were nearly a couple of yards in diameter. If we had collided with one it would certainly have sunk us right away, for it must be remembered that the metal of our floats was only about one thirty-second of an inch thick and, although they could take severe shocks when the whole surface hit the water, a sudden blow at any particular spot would puncture them immediately. We landed on the water and taxied up to one of the buoys at the extreme end and just managed to get alongside without any trouble, but unfortunately when we had been tied up the wash of the river bumped us on to the buoy and bent one float a little. Only very slight damage was done, but we realised that it must not occur again. The moment we pulled up, scores of native craft put out from the shore to get a closer view of us. Every native boatman who had a craft of any sort made his fortune that day, for he simply crammed his boat with masses of native passengers until it was on the verge of sinking, then endeavoured to row them round our machine. There was a terrific current running at the time – about six knots – and these foolish fellows seemed to drift down on to the machine pell-mell and then at the last moment trust to luck to steer off to the right or left and just miss crashing into our floats. I became very anxious because I knew the damage that might occur should one of these boat-loads of sight-seers collide with the seaplane, and they were absolutely out of control owing to the enormous loads they had on board and the very strong current which was far greater than they could cope with. I shouted at them with all my might to keep clear, but it was of no avail; all they did was to grin and laugh. At last I thought of the syringe with which we tested the floats for any leakage, and we proceeded to squirt every boat-load that came within reach. This was very effective for they had a strong objection to having their best white clothes spoilt by water.

Soon after landing, the Burma Oil Company lowered a barge from the bank on strong ropes with all our fuel aboard and then by a system of semi-rotary pumps our machine was filled up in twenty minutes. We stayed the night at the ancient fort that is situated at the point where the Jumna and Ganges meet. The sands below this fort are a sacred spot to the Hindu and many ceremonies are held here. My bedroom window looked out on to a small balcony which over hung the gaunt fortress walls washed by the waters of the Jumna beneath. When I looked over the balcony on that star-lit night I could see the drifting debris passing quickly down the stream fifty feet below. The walls of the fort were anything from ten to twenty feet thick and, having passed through a kind of passage from the window into the room, it was like being in an enormous cavern with solid stone walls. It was a huge apartment, at least thirty feet square. Having made sure that the machine was safe for the night, I had a last look at her from the balcony and then turned into bed. On the following morning I awoke all fresh to carry on with the job, but to my dismay found that it was pouring with rain and I knew we had at last hit the monsoon. It was hardly light at the time so I decided to make no plans regarding my start until the day had progressed a little, and then I discovered that although the storms were particularly heavy they were more or less local, and that when once I got in the air I ought to be able to dodge between them.

We got away from our moorings in a way we had found most practical on previous occasions. We let ourselves down from the buoy on a very long rope until we were trailing fifty yards behind it on the end of the rope; then we set to work to start the engine while we were held in this manner. On this occasion we had no difficulty in starting up and, the moment the propeller was ticking over, Ward cut the rope and I opened out, and then with complete control we taxied away across the river. Now it is absolutely essential to take off head into the wind no matter how light it is, especially when one has a very heavy load on board, because if the wind were blowing say at ten miles an hour and it so happened that our machine took off in still air at fifty miles an hour, it would mean that if we flew head into that wind we should take off with a forward ground speed of forty miles an hour.

The wind on the morning we left Allahabad was changeable and the last time I tried to ascertain its direction I estimated that the nearest way to get head into the wind would be to take off up-stream. This meant flying up current which, in the early stages of our take-off would possibly hinder us. However, knowing that head into wind would be best, I got into mid-stream and opened out. We went on, and on, and on, for ages, and it seemed as though we should never come off the water. The day was calm and naturally the surface of the river was smooth. At last we came unstuck and climbed away gradually, and it was not until then as we skimmed over the railway bridge, which I had doubts at one time that we should miss, that I suspected that we had taken off down wind. On turning to fly off on our course I noticed a small bonfire on the river bank and by the direction of its smoke I could see that sure enough the wind had changed and we had taken off down it.

We had a six-hundred-mile flight down the course of the Ganges to Calcutta and were successful all that time in dodging through the majority of the storms and arriving a little after midday over the Hooghli. Of course we did not hug the river the whole length of our journey. We cut off all the big corners and crossed one mountain range, but even so we were not very long out of touch of an alighting place owing to the windings of the Ganges and its many tributaries. The Hooghli is an enormous river, about a mile wide, and the spot where we had been told to land had been specially cleared for our arrival. A motor launch was in attendance so the moment we landed I taxied up to within a fair distance of it then shut off and drifted down stream; getting out our heaving lines. The launch came up and they caught our line first shot, so that a few moments later we were taken in tow. The first words our Calcutta friends got across to us were, 'Whatever you do, don't fall in, for if you do you'll never come up again'. The river was full of eddies, with a violent tidal current running as well, but greatest menace of all were the strong under-currents which, it is a known fact, will draw a man under if he happens to fall in rather deeply and he does not come up again, unless perhaps it is some miles further down where that particular current comes to the surface. Knowing Ward's aptitude for going overboard, I strictly warned him and we crept about our floats with anxious care, for after all it is no easy matter to hop along the cross-bars and climb about the swaying machine when one's shoes are slippery with oil. My old friend, Captain Scott, the station Staff Officer, was waiting on the B.O.C. launch to receive us and, as on my previous visit to Calcutta when I had landed Sir Sefton Brancker on the race course, he had made every possible arrangement and attended to every detail for our welfare and comfort. As soon as the machine was moored up to the police launch which took charge of her, we went aboard the B.O.C. launch where lunch was prepared beneath a big awning. Shaw Wallace, the B.O.C. agents, were our hosts and amid the merry gathering on board I felt that the flight was progressing after all, and though it had its trials there were also its compensations.

After spending the night at Fort William we were ready to push on again towards Akyab. The weather reports were fairly favourable and so I decided to go at once because we were getting near the Burmese coast where the monsoon is at its very worst. We had said goodbye to our friends and, owing to the ample space, had cast adrift on the river and had just started our engine up preparatory to taking off when I discovered that the rudder had jammed and would not function. The only thing to do was to shut off and shout to the launch to come and take us in tow again. Now to work on the tail of a machine when afloat is no easy matter, as it is high out of the water, but we twisted the machine round so that the tail overhung a small launch, and from this point I was able to inspect and adjust the rudder. This delayed us about half an hour but eventually we got off the water and flew eastward, north of the Sundarbans and over the many mouths of the River Ganges towards Chittagong. The first fifty miles was hardly a good seaplane route, but even so it was better for a seaplane than an aeroplane. The further east we got the more the rivers of this great delta running due south increased in number, so that we were within gliding distance of a good alighting spot almost the entire way until we came to the open sea beyond Barisal. After this we followed the coast-line round to Chittagong where we discovered another very fine seaplane base but, without landing, passed on down the Burmese coast beyond Cox's Bazaar towards Akyab. As one reaches Burma the country suddenly changes from open paddy fields and swamp, to a mountainous country of which every inch is either cultivated or is covered with the rich vegetation of the tropical jungle and forest. The weather was threatening, but we got to Akyab without any trouble and landed on a good seaplane base in a creek which I had discovered on my previous flight to Rangoon.

At Akyab we thought we would try a new system of warming the engine up. Naturally it was necessary to run our Siddeley-Jaguar a little before opening out to full throttle and taking off. It is necessary for any motor to get the oil circulated and sufficiently warmed so that the metal may expand before it has the terrific weight of full throttle thrust upon it. The usual method of warming up a seaplane engine is to taxi about over the water for a little time before taking off, but this is not always convenient as there may be no room for such a manoeuvre. So at Akyab I hit upon the idea of attaching the machine by means of a rope to the launch and then being held from behind by this rope while the engine was ticking over and warming up, and so we put our scheme into practice. All went well for a few seconds, when we noticed that the rope was gradually getting tighter and tighter, and thinner and thinner, until suddenly it snapped and we lurched forward. There was a small craft holding the line out of the water and as the rope broke close up to the seaplane, it sprang back with great violence, encircling the occupants of the rowing-boat and nearly dragging them over-board. The situation was ludicrous but we had no time to laugh or dally, so we just opened out and took off straight ahead on our way down the coast of Burma.

We had not gone very far before I was aware that we were in for a bad time and were going to hit the Burma rains that we had heard so much about. It may be of interest to mention here that whereas the average rainfall in the British Isles is about thirty inches per annum, on the Burma coastline it is anything up to three hundred inches a year and all this rain falls within a period of four or five months. These figures will give a fair conception of the quantity of rain that can fall in these regions. My course lay due south down the coast of Burma and therefore on the western side of the Arakanyoma range until I got to a point where I hoped to get over these hills at a few hundred feet into the valley of the Irrawaddy, and then fly due east to Rangoon. All went well until we suddenly found ourselves surrounded by heavy rain storms, completely overcast skies, and altogether a totally different state of affairs to the monsoons of India. We simply had to fly on, and there were moments when the rain was so dense that my visibility was reduced to about a hundred and fifty yards. Under these conditions it meant flying as slowly as possible at a very low altitude along the beach, where the coast-line was rocky and inundated with bays and inlets. The twistings and turnings required in order to maintain any sort of view ahead – as there seemed to be no visibility when one looked out over the sea – made it a most difficult and alarming task. I have memories of plunging into dark banks of rain which became blue-black as we flew deeper into the storm. So it became darker and darker and the rain became heavier every moment, and if it had not been for the fact that I was fairly confident that the heaviest of the rain was only a few miles thick I could not have gone on. But I peered hopefully ahead for a little light on the horizon and as the blackness gave way to a lighter hue I knew that the worst of that particular storm was over; and thus I gathered confidence to continue until finally we emerged into a clearer atmosphere once more.

By this time I had given up all hope of getting over the mountains and flying over the Irrawaddy to Rangoon, and was contenting myself with the prospect of making an enormous circle right round the coast-line to Burma and then flying due south up the Rangoon River to Rangoon, thus avoiding the high land. When I came to the usual spot where I had crossed the mountains on two previous occasions, they were simply buried in black clouds, so I passed on through several rain storms, until suddenly there was a big clearing in the atmosphere and at a point that was approximately due east of Rangoon itself I could see that I could pass over the hills at a low point and get into the Irrawaddy valley without fear of being caught in low clouds or storm. This was a great relief and I had soon passed over the jungle and hit up the big river, passing right over Bassein and heading straight for Rangoon, when, within about five miles of the town we encountered a rain storm of such intensity that it was literally impossible to weather it. It was a great pity to have to about turn within three or four minutes of my goal, but I did not relish flying over the tree-tops and forests north of Rangoon in a blinding storm with no visibility. So I reluctantly turned and endeavoured to make a big circle round the storm, flying southwards in this endeavour, but it was bigger than I had thought and it forced me to travel for miles and miles in a southerly direction, always keeping in touch with various rivers and canals, until at last I found myself within sight of the sea. As another big storm was coming up, I decided to land on a convenient looking creek beneath me and wait for a little for the weather to clear. There happened to be a steamer trudging its peaceful way up these quiet waters and so I thought it would be a good thing to land alongside and press it into our service, as the banks on either side of the river were very thickly wooded and it would be unpleasant to drift into them. So we alighted on the water and taxied up alongside this steamer and shouted to them to stop and throw us a line. A crowd of natives hung over the side, staring in open-mouthed wonder at our machine, but they showed no intention of slowing down, though we screamed and yelled and waved our arms frantically. Then as a last despairing effort we fired a rocket, which really seemed to impress them because I noticed that they were slowing down and that we were drifting nearer. I could not come too near, however, and I hoped they would put out a boat and take us in tow, but they were so leisurely about it that by the time they had done so we had drifted down stream until we gradually collided with the bushes that grew deep into the water along the edge of the creek. Luckily everything was very resilient and no damage was done. Then followed a period in which we endeavoured to persuade the native who had put off in the small boat to come near us with, a line so that we might be taken in tow, for it was clear to me that the steamer must pull us out of the bushes if we were to get out of the creek at all. But still the nervous native refused to come near enough to help us. It started to rain heavily, and we were quickly drenched to the skin, and before we could get the cover over the engine that was drenched too; and amid all our difficulties that stupid native just hovered about five or six yards away in his boat, not knowing what to do. For my part the grimness of the situation was relieved by Ward, who stood on the end of the float and told the native in his best Cockney what he would do to him if he once got hold of him. Then he tried to coax him, but without effect, then he shouted violently at him, and finally as the native still held off he was almost in tears. The things he said about that stupid native and what he would do to him, once aboard the skiff, would have caused the poor fellow to pass right away had he understood the language.

At last I seized an opportunity and leaped into the boat myself, after which I was quickly aboard the steamer asking for the skipper. I found he was a native, and that no one aboard could speak or understand English. It was quite a big steamer, as river craft go, carrying a cargo of petrol somewhere up-river. I showed the skipper my map and asked if I could see his, but I soon learned that he knew nothing about maps and had never seen such a thing before. However, he knew where he had come from and where he was going to, and from that I ascertained our position. It appears he had come from Rangoon, and from what I had seen of the creek before landing I estimated we were about thirty miles south of Rangoon and about ten miles west of the main river. Then by means of a rope I managed, while the steamer was anchoring in mid-stream, to haul our craft out of the bushes into safe waters, and then I made them promise they would remain at anchor and stand by while we were held in this fashion. The next move was to get aboard the seaplane again, so I jumped into the skiff once more and was quickly on the floats.

I sent the native back to the steamer and decided the only thing to do was to get off straight away. This of course meant testing the engine very severely, for the instant the motor started up it would mean opening out to full throttle if we were to get off successfully. The engine had been exposed in a heavy downpour now for over an hour and looked just as though a hose pipe had played on it. All the same we were determined to take off, and Ward proceeded to start the engine up. Our plan was that the moment we were certain the engine had started and was going to fire properly, Ward would cut us adrift and jump into the cabin as quickly as possible, whereupon I would open out and get into the air. All being ready, Ward gave me contact the moment he started to turn the hand-starting gear; she fired first time; he cut the ropes and leapt into the cabin; I opened out the throttle, and within three seconds of starting our poor old Jaguar engine, which had been icy cold and in a deluge for over an hour, it was given full throttle which it took without a murmur and we were off the water and in the air, circling over the steamer. The whole crew stood aghast and are probably talking to-day of those weird people who dropped out of the skies on to the water beside them, upset all their arrangements, caused them to stop their engines, cut their best manilla rope, and left them again without a 'thank you'.

In a few seconds we had left our steamer far behind and were heading north-east, following the course of the creek which I knew would lead into the main Rangoon River. It was late afternoon, the light was failing, and we were flying in the aftermath of a very severe storm. The skies were overcast and threatening, and rather than run the risk of being caught out in a sudden squall over a forest swamp, I followed the course of the creek in preference to a direct compass course for Rangoon. At last we struck the great Rangoon River which runs from Rangoon to the sea, and flew up this wide waterway, at the head of which we could see the port of Rangoon, until we came to Monkey Point which is looked upon as the seaplane base of the district.

CHAPTER III

RANGOON TO PORT DARWIN

The Air Survey Company had used Monkey Point as their head-quarters for two or three years but, the survey of the Irrawaddy Valley finally completed, they had gone further afield for their work, so that the entire Company happened to be in Borneo with the exception of one very good fellow who had been left behind to clear up affairs. However, many people were taking an interest in our landing, and the military and the port authorities collaborated in superintending these arrangements. When we arrived I could see no buoy, at least none in a position that I would care to approach under my own power, and so I landed well out in the river and, noticing several launches which presumably were there to render us assistance, I just switched off the engine and waited to be taken in tow. There was little activity for several minutes, during which time we were drifting towards the bank, when eventually out of the muddle of craft a little motor-launch emerged, crammed to its utmost capacity.

By this time we were drifting near the slipway and it looked as though we should collide with a mud bank on which were littered many rocks and stones. Ward and I, each seated straddle-legged on the bow-tips of our floats, our feet dangling almost in the water, were shouting for assistance to natives on the bank, urging them to jump in and hold us before we grounded on the rocks. One charming young fellow who had evidently come to assist us happened to be standing on the slipway and felt the weight of his responsibility, for he became

very agitated when he saw the wings of the machine drifting perilously near to a projecting wooden structure and our floats in such
close proximity to the rock-strewn bank; at last, with a wild yell, he
dived head first into the river and disappeared, to emerge from the
brown liquid just under my foot, within one inch of our metal floats!
By this time the natives had gained courage by our friend's example and thus we were man-handled on to the slip-way. After putting
wheels on to the floats by mean of running a long shaft through a
special axle-hole that had been made through our floats at the correct spot for balance against such an emergency, we were able, with
the assistance of scores of willing helpers, to commence hauling our
machine up the slipway. The wheels were not quite big enough, as
there was only about half an inch clearance between the bottom
of the floats and the ground, with the result that the utmost care
was necessary to prevent damage to the floats. So that perhaps our
arrival and introduction to the people of Rangoon lacked polish and
charm, in that Ward and I could only concentrate on organising the
gang of humanity that was so willing to help us. We had to take it
for granted that they were out to help us and having, assumed that,
we just bullied everyone into action. Natives were cursed at freely,
caught hold of and placed in position, and by practical demonstration
shown how either to push or hold. Europeans were commandeered
to control the natives, and anybody standing about with his hands
in his pockets, no matter who it was (and especially if he grinned
at the situation), quickly had the smile removed from his face by a
rude remark from myself requesting him to turn to and give a hand.
I meant no offence to anybody and here offer my sincere apologies
should I have hurt a soul; my only excuse is that we were up against
it. The slightest mishandling meant damage to our craft and ruin to
the expedition, and as I was determined that should get through with
the flight, and as the immediate job was to get that machine up into
the hangar, I was out to achieve my object by any means possible.

At last we were housed, our baggage taken from the machine,
and enquiries made regarding fuel supplies and natives to assist in

cleaning on the morrow (for I intended to use Rangoon as a base for the inspection and repainting of the bottom of our floats); when all these preparations had been made, very tired and very thirsty, I jumped into a car and drove into town. After a bath I was much refreshed, and while I sipped tea and ate biscuits I was able to write my dispatches for cabling to England and Australia. The moment this was done the door of my room was opened to admit the flood of local press correspondents. Having satisfied the exhaustive enquiries of these kind gentlemen, I was able to get down to general corre-spondence, the writing up of reports upon the engine and machine, the entering up of log-books and the cabling of our immediate movements, past and present, to various points along the route, and thus more or less completed the general routine of the day.

After a clear day in Rangoon, during which we had inspected and repainted our floats, cleaned the machine, had a thorough look over controls and attended to odd details of our engine, we were fortunate in waking to find a moderately fine day for our next jump to Victoria Point. We followed the same procedure in letting our aircraft down the slipway into the water as we had in drawing it up, and eventu-ally we were ready to take off. On the first part of our flight our course lay almost due east out over the open sea across to Moulmein, and then our route lay southward following the coast-line of Burma. We arrived over Moulmein just after a severe rain-storm. There was a break in the clouds and the sun was shining, giving us a beauti-ful vision of the many pagodas and the oriental splendours of the temples standing out clearly as the sun shone on the glistening wet-ness of their golden roofs. The skies were generally overcast and the horizon was never exactly clear, but nevertheless there was beauty in this mountainous jungle and forest-clad coast line. Every rock that protruded from the sea, so long as it was possible for a seed of any sort to rest on its precipitous walls, was covered with a blanket of rich green vegetation. Even on the smallest rock-islands trees and creepers grew abundantly right down to the water's edge, and where the rock did not enter sheer into the sea there would invariably be a little silver-sand beach which separated the water from the jungle. It was of course the monsoon period and the water was not very clear but, from my previous experience of the coast of Burma at another time of the year, I knew how wonderful the scenery could be when the skies were gloriously blue and the land was bathed in sunshine. Out of the monsoon period the waters are so clear that from an altitude one can look right through the ocean to its bed in fathoms of water and it is difficult to tell exactly where the surface of the water begins.

We flew for about a hundred miles, and then went inland over a rocky cliff for just a few miles until we came to Tavoy, where we followed the great Tavoy River which runs parallel to the coast line until at last it breaks into the open sea. Later we passed over the town of Mergui, but it was a dull day with low clouds and I was worried during most of the flight lest I might be caught out in bad weather and forced to land and take refuge from heavy rain. About fifty miles from Victoria Point the skies cleared and the sun shone, so that before leaving the Mergui Archipelago, which consists of over nine hundred islands through which we had been finding our way ever since we left Tavoy, it could be seen at its best. I should imagine that even the most unromantic soul could hardly fail to be moved by the scores of beautiful islands over which we passed. One felt how delightful it would be to land in some of these sheltered bays, to float quietly on the clear blue water and linger awhile in the gentle breezes of so delectable a climate. But we had a job to do and, what was more, there were no supplies for us until we got to Victoria Point, nearly six hundred miles from Rangoon; so we cruised quietly on until at last this V-shaped prominence, which is the southernmost point of Burma and the very end of the Indian Empire, came into view. At Victoria Point the scenery is delightful and, apart from the luxuriant tropical vegetation and the wonderful clearness of the atmosphere, one might imagine oneself in the Lake District at home. We lost no time in landing and, finding that our moorings were in a very strong current, I taxied into the lee of an island just off the shore, threw out our own anchor and waited in these quiet waters while our good friends shifted the mooring for us.

I think that everybody knows that the Siddeley-Jaguar engine we were using on this flight was the identical motor that took me with the late Mr A. B. Elliott from London to Cape Town and back. Now I can always remember that before starting on that Cape flight, when arranging as to what spare parts we should carry, one of the managers at the Armstrong-Siddeley Works seemed reluctant that we should carry spare valve-springs. He maintained that these had never been known to break and it was therefore quite unnecessary. On the other hand I maintained that valve-springs were a part of the mechanism of an aircraft engine, no matter what make, and in time were liable to break, especially after considerable running. So I had my way and we carried a few springs on the Cape flight, though I was glad to find that they were never required. This performance evidently gave the Armstrong-Siddeley manager confidence, so that after the Jaguar had been overhauled we set out for the great Australian flight with the same valve-springs that had taken us to the Cape and back. Now with valve-springs it is purely a matter of time for the metal to become tired and the temper to go, so that at last they break. It must be remembered that on both flights we had been subjected to severe extremes of heat and cold, and so when on arrival at Akyab we had found one spring broken I was not surprised. Out of the three spare springs that we were carrying it had been quickly renewed – a matter of about minutes' work. Then at Rangoon we found that another spring had gone, and I naturally became a little disturbed. However this one also had been renewed and we had set out for Victoria Point. As we neared our destination I noticed that the engine was not running as smoothly as when we had started, and that she needed just a little more throttle than usual; having tested the ignition on the separate switches, I knew that it could not be either plug or magneto trouble. I therefore surmised that our clearances wanted a little adjusting, and on landing I told Ward about it. Curiously he had not noticed anything wrong with the motor, but the moment we started to inspect the engine we soon found the cause of the trouble. Instead of another spring having broken there were no less than six gone. Mr J. D. Siddeley, who had fathered this flight, told me that the Jaguar would never let me down, and I relate this little incident because surely no other engine in the world than a Jaguar could have carried on so well and with so little ill-effect with six valve-springs broken; I appreciated anew the old saying that no matter what happens, the Jaguar will always get you there somehow.

Now we had only one spare spring left and this meant a set of inner and of outer springs, so we had to search round to find others at Victoria Point. Our friends even sent over to Ranawng, a village on the Siamese coast, where they managed to find three odd springs from an old Thornycroft marine engine. Then we found one or two bits of odd motor springs, and by splitting up our remaining spares so that we had valves running on a single inner spring and a single outer spring, we managed somehow to fix the engine up so that all valves had a spring of some sort. When we came to leave Victoria Point our engine started up, ran perfectly and gave full revolutions.

We had a delightful cruise from Victoria Point to Penang, and once we were one hundred and fifty miles south of Victoria Point I knew we were finally out of the monsoon area. We were fortunate in having a perfect day, and if the Mergui Archipelago had been beautiful, the islands along this coast line were even more wonderful still. I noted many seaplane harbours on my run down, and as it transpired it was lucky that I did so, because through these little observations I knew where to fly for shelter on the return journey.

About five o'clock in the afternoon we came into Penang harbour just as the sun was going down behind the mountain at the back of the town, so that the clear-cut rock horizon formed by the mountain stood out boldly, illuminated by the great light behind it. We landed in the bay, which was quite calm, and as we could find no mooring we heaved our own little anchor overboard. We discovered that we had come quicker than our telegram and they had been unprepared for us; for it appeared they dared not leave our mooring out, having already had three stolen by the native fishermen during the fortnight that they had been expecting our arrival. However they soon brought out an anchor and we were quickly tied up in calm waters.

Somehow I experienced a feeling of relief on arrival here, for from all the accounts that I could gather we ought to have nothing but fine weather before us for the rest of our journey to Australia.

Penang was the start of public functions (very often the hardest work on a flight of this nature) for that evening, immediately the machine had been fixed up for the night and the Port Officer had kindly undertaken to look after Ward, I motored off with the Governor to Government House.

Penang is a delightful town, deservedly noted for its perfect order and cleanliness. As we left the centre of the city we passed through broad, spacious avenues overhung with magnificent trees. Everywhere there seemed to be abundance of foliage in which the villas of the merchants of Penang were partially hidden. Government House here is perhaps one of the most beautiful in the whole of the East, with imposing views of the great mountain behind the town appearing above the Residency lawns. It was a wonderful moonlit night and I longed to rest in this delightful spot, instead of which I had to dress in a matter of minutes and dash off with the Governor to an important dinner where, he told me, my presence was very much requested.

The following morning we wended our way most reluctantly down to the bay to continue our big journey. Our mooring was very close in to the shore and, fearing that in the gentle breeze I might have some difficulty in turning the machine out to sea without colliding with some rocks close at hand, I decided it would be safest to be towed out a little way. I imagined that a native rowing a sampan could easily do this job. There was little current and very little wind, so we simply unhitched and the sampan took our line. But we soon discovered that the native, however hard he rowed, had no power whatever to tow us. We then called to another sampan for

Above and below: At every step throughout Australia, Cobham and Ward were required to attend lunches, dinners and public gatherings. Almost all were formal events which put a severe strain on the crew's limited wardrobe.

assistance, and in tandem fashion these two endeavoured to move us. But even they could not manage the job; we only seemed to go round in circles. Then at last we commandeered a third sampan and thus, with three sampans rowing in line, they just managed to tow our craft out to sea over calm waters. This is the more remarkable when it is remembered that it is possible for a strong swimmer to push our seaplane about unaided, provided there is no current against him. I think the failure of the sampans was due to the fact that they draw no water at all and consequently have no way on. Once we were a couple of hundred yards from the shore we cast our tugs – or tuggers – aside, started up the engine and quietly taxied into a convenient position for our take-off.

There is a great fascination about sea-going aircraft, whether it be seaplane or flying-boat, especially if the waters are calm, when it is possible to cruise along like a fast motor-boat, and to know at the same time that you have sufficient power to leave the water and cruise in the air if you feel so inclined.

As soon as we were in a convenient position I turned the nose of our de Havilland into the wind, opened out, and took off. Our next jump was a matter of some four hundred miles to Singapore and was more or less uneventful, except that the coast line was full of interest. The huge cocoa-nut and rubber plantations that we passed over were specially interesting. There was one cocoa-nut plantation that was set out in regular rows and rectangular formation and, with the exception of the necessary roadways and canals, it was one vast forest of palms that extended for about twenty miles along the coast and at least ten or fifteen miles inland. I understand that cocoa-nut palms must be grown in close proximity to the sea, and that they rarely do any good more than fifty miles away from it.

At Penang, after our flight from Victoria Point with the odd valve-springs, we discovered that all the temporary ones that we had fixed up were holding good, but that two more of the original ones had broken, so that we had to patch up again with two chance motor-springs. In this somewhat tied-up condition we once more took off on the four-hundred-mile journey, but knowing that when we reached Singapore we should find spare parts which had been shipped there from our previous organisation in Africa and that we could therefore renew these springs throughout the engine. In due course we were flying over Singapore and landing in the harbour opposite the Yacht Club. We were extremely surprised to see the interest that was evinced in our arrival by the goodly throng that had assembled to meet us.

Conditions for the seaplane were now becoming ideal, for as at Penang, we just landed on calm waters, shut off our engine, and awaited the motor launch which a few moments later came alongside and took us in tow. At the same time an anchor strong enough to hold a steam-ship was cast for us in a convenient spot at our own direction. These little affairs were easily dealt with and soon we had stepped on the launch and were being received at the pier by the Colonial Secretary. A few moments later we were sitting on the lawns of the Yacht Club which overlook the harbour where, about two hundred yards away, our seaplane was swinging gently in the breeze.

There had been a question, before starting this flight, as to whether or not we should carry dress clothes. With the extra weight of floats and our huge petrol capacity, I had considered casting aside dress formalities and refusing all invitations to public functions, just getting down to the actual job of the flight alone. But at the last moment (knowing well what our various kind hosts would be) we decided to put in a dinner jacket and a couple of shirts. Therefore I was O.K. at Penang and again at Singapore, but Ward who, it will be remembered, had joined me from the Air Force at Basra at a moment's notice, had only just time to cast off his uniform and push what few civilian clothes he had into a bag before we started. At Singapore we were separated for the night, and when I heard of the dinner in our honour I was a little perturbed on Ward's account and even sent a message explaining the difficulty. Imagine then my surprise on arriving at the function to find Ward, immaculate in dress kit, making me feel quite shabby beside him! I noticed at dinner that he sat very upright, with shoulders squared, but I learned afterwards that there was a sinister reason for his splendid carriage, for he confessed next day that he had been scared stiff that some of the pins that had been so lavishly employed in fixing him in his borrowed suit would come away!

A whole day was spent at Singapore in looking over our engine and machine. I found it most difficult to ascertain anything definite about the weather in these regions. There seemed to be no rule as to when the rain might come, and there seemed to be no seasons. During the whole year the temperature at Singapore is invariably somewhere between 80 and 90 degrees Fahrenheit, and the rain so far as I could make out might come at any time. One might have a storm early in the morning, which would clear up later in the day. On the other hand it might be clear in the morning with heavy storms in the evening. It might rain the whole night long and be fine all day, or it might pour a deluge from sunrise to sunset and be fine all night. Then again it might be misty with drizzle all day, or the same conditions might arise in the evening after a clear morning; or, as we had it on the day of during departure, drizzle and bad visibility in the early morning. The extraordinary thing was that nobody could forecast the weather for an hour. No one seemed to care what it was going to be, and, so far as I could gather, it might be anything at any moment at any time of the year. I believe, however, that with a good meteorological service and reports from certain outlying stations, the weather might be far more easy to forecast than in the British Isles.

Our next flight was a short one – a mere two hundred and seventy miles from Singapore to Muntok, on Banka Island. At Muntok there was no sheltered water and we had to land in the open roads in rather heavy breakers, and when I left the machine, after having our mooring shifted closer in to get what protection there was from the piles of the jetty, I felt somewhat worried, for the wind was increasing and the waves were tossing her about in a very violent manner. In fact I stayed quite a long time wondering what I ought to do, when I was finally forced ashore by the heavy rain and the approach of night. I was content that she would not break away from the mooring; a seaplane exerts very little pull as she swings right into the wind in a gale, offering very slight resistance as it blows straight through her.

We were now in the Dutch East Indies and were staying at the rest-house in the village, situated on a high hillock overlooking the sea. The situation would have been delightful but for the heavy rain which kept us indoors. Somewhat worried, I turned into bed about eleven. According to Ward I must have had a bad nightmare about 2 a.m. I woke him with a shout, entreating him to throw the anchor out as the house was adrift, and evidently I took quite a lot of pacifying on this point.

On the following morning the sea was a little calmer and, after saying goodbye to our Dutch friends and experiencing a rather bumpy departure, we found ourselves once more in the air, flying down the Sumatra coast line towards Java. The Sumatra coast, between Banka and the island of Java on its eastern shores, runs directly north and south and is one long, lonely, desolate swamp, fringed with heavy tropical forest which is partially flooded by the sea at every high tide. For three hundred miles along this coast we did not see a sign of life, with the exception of about three odd native fishing huts. These huts are built on high piles or rickety-looking sticks which stand out about twelve to fifteen feet above the water of the mud flats along the coast. Evidently it is safer to live out over the shallow waters along the coast than in the dense jungle on the land. I noticed that it was more inclined to rain over the forest lands than out over the sea and that the low clouds, which seemed to hang right over the tree tops as we followed the coast line, ended suddenly with the beach, so that it appeared as if these banks of drifting mist were formed by the tropical jungle itself. At one point they lay heavy in the air about a hundred feet above the trees, and every few hundred yards there seemed to be a pillar of mist rising out of the forest and drifting upwards into the cloud above, so that one had the impression of thousands of bonfires all over the jungle. It was fortunate that this phenomenon ended suddenly with the sea-border, for it would have been most difficult to have flown through the mist, as in many cases the clouds came down to the tree-tops themselves.

At last we came to the point where we had to cross over the open sea to the island of Java, and when within about fifty miles of Batavia the weather suddenly changed and I could tell that we had flown into a permanent fine-weather zone. At Batavia we landed in the harbour, in the corner of which is a small seaplane base belonging to the Dutch authorities. We had a wonderful reception, as at every place in the Dutch East Indies, and as it was midday we were in time to motor in to lunch with the British Consul. It was Sunday, and, as on the Continent at home, the day was a general holiday. I was greatly struck by the gaiety of the Javanese, and more so that evening when after a dinner held in our honour we adjourned for a few minutes to the dance that was in progress at the hotel, to find that these people mix comparatively freely with their European administrators.

My route now lay due east along the great chain of islands that extends to Timor and beyond, and I was greatly impressed on our journey the following day by the intensity of the cultivation on the island of Java. It is a most prosperous country with, I understand, some forty or fifty millions of inhabitants, though the island is only about the same size as Great Britain.

From Batavia we flew eastward along the coast of Java, above a chain of great sugar-loaf mountains towering thousands of feet up, nearly all of which are extinct volcanoes; in fact it seemed that every one had been a volcano at one time or other. At some spots extinct volcanoes were standing high out of the sea, forming islands, and from our high altitude we could see that in their craters beautiful lakes had formed.

At last we came to Surabaya, at the eastern end of the island of Java, where there is a vast expanse of shallow water; but despite the fact that we only draw about six inches of water our good friends must have thought that we drew about six feet for they placed our moorings at least a mile from the shore, so that we had to be towed this distance to the hangars of the seaplane base, which I believe is the main station for the Dutch Indies Air Force. After this little yachting cruise on the end of two tow-ropes, we came alongside the jetty and were received by the Commandant who had staged a magnificent welcome for us.

On our next jump from Surabaya we flew via Bali to the island of Bima. At Bali a volcano was in partial eruption and although we tried to take photographs of the vast clouds of heavy smoke which were emitted from the mountain top, we were unsuccessful. It is interesting to note that the people of the island of Bali are of the Hindu faith and evidently emigrated here from the north, centuries ago. The natives I understand are very clever people, and very prosperous.

All day long the sun shone in cloudless skies and, although the visibility was not as great as I had anticipated, we could always see twenty or thirty miles ahead. The main wind was blowing from the south-east and as we flew along the north shores of these islands we were protected from its greatest force. It was only when we crossed from one island to another that we felt the full breeze which whipped the sea into foam-crested waves in all the various straits.

At Bima our landing-ground had been marked in a very enclosed inland water and I anticipated from its appearance on the map that we should land on a dead calm lake. But I discovered on arriving that owing to the down-current from the mountains, although our base was completely protected from the sea, there was quite a severe chop on it. However, this did not worry us but simply made it a little difficult for re-fuelling while the machine was rocking at anchor.

I have rather bitter memories of Bima, because the petrol supplies had been put down in sixteen-gallon cans! There is nothing more calculated to try the temper than to struggle with a can of fuel far too heavy for one's strength, and after narrowly missing falling into the water with it, to spill it all over the machine.

At Bima we spent the night in the rest-house, some way inland, because the native village was liable to malaria. We were about to depart on the following morning when our host insisted that we should go and see what he called the dragons. It appears that upon an island named Komodo, which is due east of Bima, there exists today a land-lizard which is to be found nowhere else in the world. The reptile is undoubtedly pre-historic and varies in length from anything up to twenty feet. At least, twenty-two feet is the longest ever seen by white men, although the natives declare that beasts thirty feet and over are quite common. These lizards are treacherous creatures which live chiefly on the wild hog, ponies and buck that abound on the island of Komodo, but should meat be short they will eat grass, palm-leaves or any other form of vegetation. They sit up on their tails in the most terrifying manner, just like the imaginary pictures so often seen of prehistoric reptiles. They can also run at an incredible speed and catch their prey, which they tear to pieces with their hands, each finger of which has a terrific talon. It is quite common for these claw-hands to be a foot across, with talons six inches long. I learned from my Dutch friend that when they have dismembered their victims, they swallow the portions whole. An American expedition had just visited the island with the object of catching these giant land-lizards alive, but although they caught many they were finally able to get only about eight specimens away, four of which went to New York, while the remaining four were given to the Dutch authorities. Two of these I understand were sent home to the Amsterdam Zoo and two were destined for the Zoo at Surabaya. I had the good fortune to see the latter two in captivity at Bima, and the larger of these was about fifteen feet in length. They were certainly the most loathsome creatures I have ever seen.

It was extraordinary to find how much stir was caused by my dispatch about the Dragons of the Island of Komodo, and how every newspaper made them grow day by day. In fact, one of the leading papers in Rangoon had a gigantic headline stretched across the whole sheet which told of land-lizards ninety yards long, while fifty and a hundred feet were very common speculations of quite conservative papers.

From Bima we continued our journey eastward, this time flying south of the island of Flores to the island of Rotti, until at last Timor came on the horizon. Ever since we left Sumatra we had been flying against a steady head wind and I was glad to learn that the same wind would be blowing on our return journey, so that whereas it had been a disadvantage on the outward trip we should have the benefit of a following wind on the homeward flight. On this part of the journey we constantly passed over shoals of whales, and in the clear waters beneath us from a thousand feet we often saw weird giant fish of which I was never able to give a good enough description for identification because we were not low enough for close observation.

With the naked eye we had magnificent views of the ocean bed through many fathoms of water, but somehow the camera seemed unable to capture all that we could see. Owing to the general roughness of the sea in the open roads at Kupang we landed in a little bay a few miles to the south, at Tani, and here we found that the Dutch authorities had most courteously placed one of their government steamships at our disposal. As we approached we could see S.S. *Gemma* lying at anchor, and between the steamer and the shore was the red oil-drum with a hook on top which was our mooring. After circling round the steamship, which appeared to be crammed full of ladies, we landed on the water and taxied up to our mooring, which Ward successfully hooked from the float-side.

Aboard the *Gemma* there seemed to be the entire population of Kupang. Our arrival had been made the occasion of a general holiday and, by the kind permission of the Commodore, everyone was having a joy-trip.

I do not think the ladies in that part of the world had seen much aircraft before, and probably looked upon an aviator as a kind of super-being, or an inhuman monster. All I know is that it was most embarrassing when, after climbing up the gangway and shaking hands with the captain, I found four scores of pairs of feminine eyes centred unwaveringly upon me. After the little reception was over we were allowed to wash, change and make ourselves more or less respectable, and later in the afternoon, while Ward went back to the seaplane to prepare for the next day's flight, we steamed up to Kupang to drop our load of sightseers. It was during this little voyage that I had ample time to prepare my dispatches, and later on still more time for getting up my vast arrears of correspondence and reports.

Our next flight was to be the longest jump over the sea of the whole journey, for after leaving the island of Timor we had nearly five hundred miles of ocean to cross before we came to Australia.

Naturally we were quite confident about our engine and machine and we knew that unless anything very unforeseen happened it was highly improbable that they would let us down. Really all that had to be done was to steer a good compass course and resign ourselves to a few monotonous hours of flying out of sight of land, relying on our compass to bring us eventually to our destination.

I had arranged that our departure and arrival should be watched at each end of this passage; at Kupang the Dutch authorities were going to wireless to the receiving station at Darwin the time of our departure, also the compass bearing that we were going to take over the sea.

At Kupang a long cable was waiting for me from Colonel Brinsmead, the Director of Civil Aviation in Australia, informing me that on receipt of news of our departure from Kupang, HMS *Geranium* of the Royal Australian Navy, would watch our flight over the sea and, if we did not arrive at Darwin at the scheduled time, they would 'take the necessary action'. What the 'necessary action' meant I hardly knew, but the message gave us a distinct feeling of security.

So it came about that we were up soon after dawn and by 7 a.m. were in the air heading for the southern corner of the island of Timor, where we took up our compass bearing and set out over the sea.

Our instrument was perhaps the finest aeroplane compass in the world. It is known as the Hughes Aperiodic and is the result of exhaustive mathematical research and experiment during the latter years of the war. The head wind still prevailed, for we were flying right into the teeth of the south east trades, and in order to avoid the main force of this gale we flew very low; in fact our average height over the sea from Timor to Darwin must have been somewhere in the region of fifty to a hundred feet. The direction of the wind continually changed a little; first of all it would be blowing head on to us, then it would veer a bit to our port, then again it would get over to our starboard; but it was always against us, and as it veered so I allowed a few points on the compass to rectify the drift. This kept us on an approximate compass course. Owing to the fact that I had to pilot the machine, it was impossible for me to do any real navigation, for in order to navigate properly it is necessary to have an experienced navigator on board who has his hands free to do that job alone. All the navigating that I could do was to fly on a dead reckoning, having procured my bearing with a protractor on an Admiralty chart before I left Kupaug. Beyond this, any alterations that I made in that course were done purely by guess work and from a certain amount of practical experience.

When about twenty minutes had passed, the land began to fade away behind us – visibility was not very good that day – and soon we were out over the open sea, settling down and resigning ourselves to three or four hours flying towards the reliefless horizon.

First of all I calculated the shortest time in which we could do this jump; then I computed the longest time that we ought to take; and so I worked out these estimates on my watch, because I realised that if land were not sighted in a given time then my course must be too northerly, in which case I should have to fly due south to hit the Australian continent.

I had been told that the visibility might be a hundred and fifty miles, and so when a certain time had elapsed and land failed to appear in the distance I began to get a little perturbed. But after thinking the matter over I came to the conclusion that perhaps the visibility was bad that day and that therefore I must continue on my

present course until such time as I ought to see land if there were
no visibility at all. Now when this limit was reached and there was
still no sight of land the situation became very worrying, because
it meant one of two things, either that the head wind was much
stronger than I thought and was holding us back, or that we were
not steering a correct course but were perhaps drifting north of the
island of Melville. At last I decided that it must be the wind that was
holding us back, so I still held on to my original course, peering
ahead all the time to catch a glimpse of land. Several times I thought
I had sighted the distant shore, only to find that the wish had been
father to the thought, and what I had mistaken for land either disappeared as we drew nearer or turned out to be a shadow on the water
or some change in the colouring owing to a local coral reef or some
such formcation.

All this time our engine purred perfectly. Hours passed by and
our petrol got lower and lower, until I began to estimate how long
it would be before it gave out. Then again I considered how the
machine would land on the rather rough water underneath; and if it
did land safely and there was no petrol left, how long we should keep
afloat and how long we could live on the rations that we had aboard.
We did not give way to depression however, but simply kept on our
course in the belief that we should come out safely as on every previous occasion.

At last a faint shade appeared on the horizon – a dim outline with
a little kink in it which did not alter as we drew nearer – and at last
I realised that it was land ahead and shouted through to Ward to tell
him the glad news.

The coast of Australia is extremely lonely and desolate in this part
and we had no idea, if our compass course had failed, where we
might strike it. But at the moment we did not worry over that little
trifle; the great thing was that land was ahead, and so, still keeping on
our course in half-an-hour we were crossing a sandy beach backed
by red cliffs on top of which was a somewhat thick bush jungle. This
was our first sight of Australia and although it was a rather desolate

Above: Naval ratings from HMS *Geranium* prepare the DH50 for the flights over land.

Left: Alan Cobham supervises the changeover from floats to wheels at Darwin.

spot, we were extremely happy, because land of some sort was better than no land at all.

After climbing a little to get a better survey of the country we discovered that, after coming nearly five hundred miles over the open sea, for the majority of the period out of sight of land; on our dead reckoning compass course we had bit our objective, namely Herd Bay, within five miles! We then proceeded along the coastline, and after about another hundred miles the harbour of Darwin came into view and we discerned the yellow funnels of HMS *Geranium* waiting there to receive us.

We had been over six hours in the air and we heard afterwards that they had been very worried, especially because they had not liked my compass course, as the bearing I had given them missed Australia and almost missed the top of Melville Island; but this was easily understood, because they took their bearing from the town of Kupang, whereas I took mine from the southernmost point of the island of Timor.

As we alighted on the water a launch came out to meet us and we were taken on board and given a rousing welcome by the officials of Port Darwin; and a greater one still by the officers and men of the *Geranium*.

I shall never forget the kindness of the Australian Navy; for apart from the fact that they had received orders from their Government to render me assistance, every man of the crew seemed only too anxious to give me a hand and do all he could to help us during our stay in Darwin.

After a little reception on board the launch, we attended to the business of getting the machine alongside the beach, where we were going to hoist three legs above her, and with a crane lift the machine sufficiently high to enable us to slip off the floats and put the undercarriage on in their place, then lower the machine to the ground the few odd feet she was suspended in the air. Then, as an aeroplane, we were going to take off at low tide from the sandy beach and land again up on the aerodrome at the back of the town – on the very

Alan Cobham pays his respects to Captain Ross Smith who, along with his three-man crew, was the first to travel by air from England to Australia, in 1919. The monument is now identified as East Point 36 in Darwin's Aviators Park.

spot where the late Sir Ross Smith landed after his famous flight from England to Australia six years ago.

Everything worked according to plan because all arrangements had been so perfectly organised for us by Colonel Brinsmead, who had travelled by air all the way from Melbourne to Darwin to meet us. I shall always consider this a very great compliment, for the

Cobham and Ward with Colonel Brinsmead, Australia's Director of Civil Aviator, following their arrival in Darwin.

Australian Government had sent their Director of Civil Aviation nearly two thousand miles to meet us — which is the equivalent of the British Government sending Sir Sefton Brancker to some point five hundred miles beyond Constantinople to meet an air voyager on the way to England!

CHAPTER IV

AUSTRALIA

We wheeled our machine up the beach on improvised wheels which were threaded on a shaft of iron. The ends were slipped into the axle-housing through our floats and then three tall scaffold poles were erected above the craft, and in this manner we hoisted her. In a short time we had taken the floats off, fitted the under-carriage and wheels in their place and converted our seaplane into an aeroplane. Colonel Brinsmead had brought with him Inspector Howard of the Civil Aviation Department, a most competent aeronautical engineer who gave us valuable help.

We towed the floats round the bay to the quay-side where HMS *Geranium* hoisted them from the water high over her decks and landed them on the jetty, where I had a railway truck waiting with batons across the top to receive the floats as they were lowered. Then we pushed the truck away with its precious load on top to the extreme end of the pier-head to wait for our return.

The weather was hot, and the fact that we were working about eighteen hours a day, we were full of high spirits because we had just accomplished the first portion of our flight. We anticipated no bad weather ahead until we were beyond Darwin on the homeward flight.

Our immediate route was to be right through Northern Territory to Queensland, then through New South Wales and on to Victoria. Our first day's jump was from Darwin due south over the bush to a place called Katherine, where we landed in a rather rough clearing to refuel. I am afraid the inhabitants were a little upset because we did not stay to lunch, but as we were already rather behind time and the journey was so short from Darwin to Katherine we could not afford the time to stay and pushed on immediately for Newcastle Waters.

Once we left Katherine we were dependent on the telegraph line to bring us up on our destination, for the road was hardly visible through the bush. Not having travelled over this part of the world before, I did not realise that the telegraph lines could not be seen at all from an altitude, as the thin metal posts were invisible, and it was the clearing in the bush through which the telegraph line ran that was going to be the visible land mark for me to follow. In due course we arrived at Newcastle Waters and it was just a toss up whether I could reach Brunette Downs before sunset; and so, after circling round Newcastle Waters for some minutes in an endeavour to find the correct track to Brunette, and thereby wasting a considerable amount of time, I decided to land at Newcastle for the night.

I was learning that, although I knew something about map-reading and a little bit about navigation, a course in path-finding would have been more useful for the back regions of Australia. There are no real maps of this part of the world, at least, not in the sense that an English surveyor would understand.

It must be remembered that we were now in one of the loneliest parts of Australia; I suppose we were as far 'out back' as one could possibly get. It was a place where living was too hard for women-folk – or at least it was allowed to remain too hard for them to exist there.

Soon after our machine came to rest on the aerodrome an old car jolted out from the huts near by to meet us. We found that the local postmaster was the man in charge, and the local police sergeant also came upon the scene. Before long we had around us a dozen or so companions who all seemed extremely interested in the machine, although I could not help noticing at the same time that conversation did not exactly flow; one word in Newcastle Waters seemed to serve the purpose of two or three hundred in any other part of the world. So there was a great deal of unusual silence after we landed, and Ward and I set to work to refuel the machine. But when we started to carry the heavy cans of petrol which had been roughly stored under some bushes near by, our new friends came forward readily – still without a word – and helped. Then I asked the postmaster whether it would be possible for us to get a shake-down for the night. He said 'Aye'. So I got our bags out of the machine and asked my silent friend whether we might beg a lift in one of the cars (there were two on the scene) down to the farm. As I stood with a bag in each hand he simply looked at me, jerked his head towards the rear car, which I took for an invitation and got inside. It was somewhat unusal perhaps, but I began to appreciate these tacit gentlemen and reflected on what an unnecessary amount of chatter goes on in our everyday life in the big cities. Certainly it was a wonderful rest cure.

We found ourselves in a shanty made of a few wooden piles supporting a tin roof, with hexagon wire around. A long table covered with a piece of linoleum ran down the centre, on which were half a dozen tin plates, while in the middle there were three Tate sugar boxes turned upside down. A few moments later three or four sturdy looking men rolled into the shelter, lifted their feet over the form and sat down. Then the postmaster took his seat at one end of the table and another robust looking fellow, dressed merely in a singlet and slacks, who apparently filled the role of cook to the party, sat at the other end of the table. Ward and I had the plank on the remaining side of the table to ourselves. As the three Tate sugar boxes were lifted from the table I realised that they were improvised dish-covers, for underneath them were three dishes of food, to which there was a mighty rush of flies. We all received helpings from the postmaster's hands and everyone took it in silence. As each man finished he handed up his plate for more, and was replenished by the postmaster without a word; and as each man finished his meal he rose and departed in absolute silence, so that within a short while we were alone with the postmaster.

We slept well that night, for luckily there was a store of new blankets from which Ward and I were supplied and therefore we were very warm in spite of the fact that there were quarter-inch gaps between the logs of our cabin walls. In the early morning it was extremely cold, but the air was fine and fresh when we wended our way down to the landing ground, started up our engine and said goodbye to our kind and silent friends.

Then we headed on our way, taking the path they told us would lead to Brunette Downs. My impression of Newcastle Waters was that here were men living out in the wilds and roughing it all unnecessarily; for little or no extra expense they could live so pleasantly. However, I discovered that this is one of the problems which is fast dying out in Australia because the coming generation demands a higher standard of living, compatible with the general advancement of the world.

We found it impossible to fly on a compass course over Northern Territory, because there was no definite feature to come out on at the end of the journey, with the exception perhaps of a small town which could very easily be missed on the vast open rolling plains of northern Australia. Furthermore there were no maps which were sufficiently accurate to follow, and the only way in which one could find one's way really successfully on a first flight over this country was by following the car tracks from place to place. This is extremely difficult the first time one goes over a route but, owing to the tremendous visibility and the ease with which one familiarises various points along the way, a second trip is rendered very simple. In fact after a fair amount of flying in Australia one develops a sense of direction which makes aerial navigation in that vast continent one of the easiest things in the world.

We soon got to Brunette Downs, the headquarters of one of the biggest cattle stations in the world. The moment we landed on a clearing near the house a car dashed out to meet us. The whole country almost the entire way from Newcastle to Brunette is one huge natural aerodrome. The roads consist of tracks over the open plains, on which, once they have been fairly well cleared, it is possible to do anything from sixty to eighty miles an hour in the right sort of car.

From Brunette we continued our journey to Camooweal, and when we came to Alexandra Station, which I believe is one of the three largest cattle-stations in the world, we discovered about ten different tracks leading southward, whereas on my rough map I had only two tracks marked. Owing to the fact that the cattle had stamped all round the station it was impossible to tell which was a car track and which a cattle track. After starting down one track I soon sensed by its general direction that it was wrong, and then started on another which in its turn dribbled away to nothing. At a third attempt I hit the right track which lead me on towards Camooweal but even so, rather than go too far out of my direction, when I espied a car coming towards us I took advantage of the wonderful country-side and just landed near by and ascertained from the occupants whether I was on the right route or not. It was a novel experience, this of being able to land anywhere at any moment, and after a cheery little chat with the two stalwart fellows in the car we said goodbye, and as they pursued their way northwards we took off again and flew southwards.

Camooweal is just in Queensland, a little town fighting its way in the out-regions of Australia. It happened to be the terminus of the famous QANTAS air route, and thus we found someone waiting on the aerodrome to give us any assistance we might require with our machine.

That night a dance was given in our honour. It was a very happy gathering of wonderful people, because despite the grim pioneer work and general hardships of the life they were leading so far away from all the amenities of modern civilisation, they seemed far more alive to the real possibilities of Australia than almost any other people I met, and I have come to the conclusion that it is the folk who live in these out-back towns of Australia who are the real back-bone of this great continent.

From Camooweal we continued our journey in the attempt to fly the whole length of the QANTAS air route in one day, and we passed right over the mining district and mountainous area towards Cloncurry. This was the first time since reaching Australia that we had passed over hilly or mountainous country and it was precisely at this point that my engine spluttered for the first time. I looked below on nothing but strewn rocks and forbidding gullies, and then there was another splutter. It was rather disturbing, but I concluded that owing to the sudden change in the atmosphere, condensation in the petrol pipes had resulted in a few spots of water getting through to the carburetter jet, but so long as it was not too bad it would soon clear itself. I think there were two more splutters after that, and then we heard no more, and fairly early in the morning we landed on the first-class aerodrome at Cloncurry where a great crowd gathered to meet us.

Sydney demanded that we should arrive there on a certain date, and I had promised to comply. So after refuelling at Cloncurry, we had very reluctantly to push on to our next stop without delay if we wished to reach Charleville before nightfall.

We had a wonderful flight from Cloncurry to Longreach, passing over flat, open, rolling plains; but it was heart-rending to see these vast areas absolutely brown and dried up, for this year they have suffered one of the greatest droughts in the history of Queensland. Day by day increasing numbers of sheep were dying, not from want of water – for owing to the wonderful engineering improvements and the efficient system of artesian wells, water is available for the animals – but the poor creatures were dying of starvation. So far as they possibly could, farmers were gallantly providing their sheep with hay purchased at an enormous cost, and with grim smiles they were watching their life's work being ruined and wondering what would be left to help them start all over again, at the end of the drought.

At Longreach there was another quick refuel. Here too were the headquarters of the QANTAS air route and what was more, a small aircraft works where they were building our own type of aeroplane under license from the de Havilland Company.

From Longreach we flew on down the line towards Charleville. It was now getting late in the day and for the last hundred miles our route lay over a vast forest with no tracks and no landmarks whatever.

Prior to reaching this forest we had passed over numerous large herds of kangaroo, evidently driven into this district by the drought. I can well remember that in one herd there were three or four hundred. The remarkable thing was that, whereas when we had flown low over herds of animals in other parts of the world they always galloped away from us, the kangaroo herds always galloped towards the machine. Whether this is curiosity or a form of fear I do not know.

The sun was sinking fast and still no sign of Charleville; nothing all round us but thick forest. Ward was looking anxious and I was feeling it, because I had to rely entirely upon my compass to hit our destination. It had not been a very long compass course – something, under a hundred miles – and I felt sure I was on the right track, but still no sign of Charleville. According to my watch we ought to have been there. The sun was getting lower and lower and I estimated about twenty minutes more daylight. I was just beginning to make up my mind that I should have to land on the first fairly open space I could find and risk wrecking the machine, as it would be very foolish to continue flying in the dark with the forest beneath, when suddenly, without any warning, we came upon the town buried in the forest about a quarter of a mile ahead, and before we had realised it we were flying over Charleville. It happens that the trees surrounding the town are very tall and the houses are rather low-built so that from a fairly low altitude Charleville cannot be seen until the aircraft is practically over it.

We soon landed on the aerodrome and were greeted by an enthusiastic crowd, many of whom had motored over bush tracks for anything from a hundred to two hundred miles to see our machine. I quickly learnt in Australia that the people of that country think nothing of distance.

That day we had flown about eight hundred and twenty five miles, and so we thought we should easily be able to keep our appointment with Sydney – over seven hundred miles away – on the next day.

That night we were entertained by the town and I was struck more than ever with the enterprise and tenacity of purpose of the people in these smaller towns of Australia. It so happened that we had overtaken Colonel Brinsmead and Captain Jones who had flown on ahead of us from Darwin, so that we had another evening together in Charleville. Next day we were up early, as both machines were destined for a long flight. Colonel Brinsmead's was a de Havilland 50 machine exactly the same as ours, but was fitted with a two hundred and thirty horse-power Siddeley Puma engine. Incidentally this is more or less the standard type of machine used throughout all the Australian air-routes, such as the Western Australian Air Way which runs from Perth to Broome right along the Western coast; the Larkin air route from Adelaide via Hay to Sydney; and the QANTAS Air-route from Camooweal to Charleville, over which we had just flown. Colonel Brinsmead intended to fly from Charleville to Melbourne in a day – a matter of nearly a thousand miles – and so naturally he had to be away at dawn. We watched Jones take off with Colonel Brinsmead and Inspector Howard as passengers, amid a terrific cloud of red dust for Charleville aerodrome is on bare red soil without any turf whatever.

On the way to our next stop, Bourke, I noticed that as we got further south the country changed from open plains or forests to vast cultivated areas, marked out in immense, oblong blocks whose boundaries run two or three miles in each direction. These huge farms were mostly for crops and from a great altitude the ground beneath looked like a huge patch-work quilt of regular pattern.

The country became greener and greener as we flew south, until at last, apart from unusual species of trees here and there, it was possible to imagine ourselves flying over Lincolnshire at home.

After a quick fill up at Bourke we took off again on a short run to Narrowmine, where we had been asked to land on the polo-ground.

Here we found a happy throng to meet us and were taken into the town for a hasty lunch, for I had promised to arrive in Sydney by 5 p.m. that afternoon. The polo-ground had a perfect surface and taking off from this beautiful green sward reminded me very much of home.

Although we had received dozens of telegrams from towns in New South Wales inviting us to fly over them on our way to Sydney, the zig-zag course we should have had to have taken to obligate everybody would have delayed our arrival by several hours, so we just had to push out on a direct route right over the Blue Mountains.

I think the flight from Narrowmine to Sydney was one of the most beautiful of the whole trip. Passing well north of Bathurst we converged with that rocky mountain range at Lithgow, where the scenery was simply perfect. When I looked at my watch I found we were going to be an hour before time. This was due to a very strong west wind which was blowing us along at a terrific speed at four or five thousand feet. The wind was at least thirty or forty miles an hour and as we were cruising at a hundred miles an hour air-speed, our speed over the ground must have been about a hundred and forty miles an hour.

Now I knew it would be disastrous to arrive at Sydney an hour before time as preparations had been made by the Aero Club of Sydney to receive us. So Ward and I amused ourselves with dallying over the Blue Mountains, taking photographs first of one glorious view then of another – not one of which was successful, however, as it was late in the afternoon and the light was thin. Moreover a special camera lens is necessary to cut the blue haze which is peculiar to these mountains and which gives them their name.

I understood that an escort was going to meet us somewhere over Richmond, and so I flew about for quite a long time waiting for it to pick us up. During this time we circled over the wonderful harbour of Sydney with all its beautiful inland waters, while away to the south we could see Botany Bay and the point where Captain Cook had first stepped ashore and discovered Australia.

These pages: Aerial views of Sydney in 1926 – before the harbour bridge was built.

Then we flew back towards Richmond in search of our escort, but evidently we were too early and I should have gone on waiting had not a single Air Force machine appeared on the horizon, circled once, and set off in the direction of Sydney, some twenty miles away, and it was not until later that I heard that a few minutes after we left the real escort of several machines turned up and was unable to find us.

At Sydney a huge crowd had gathered on the ground and the moment we landed they surrounded the machine. The police were able to cope with these kindly folk who were giving us such an enthusiastic welcome, but somehow there arose a difference of opinion amongst the press photographers, with the result that in a few minutes there was a free fight raging. One could hear the cracking of tripods as they were broken in the scrum, and how it all ended I do not now. However, after a little while matters simmered down and the Mayor of Mascot was allowed to read a wonderful address, after which our machine was pushed into the hangar and we proceeded to a public reception in the town hall of Mascot.

We spent four whole days in Sydney during which time I was chiefly under the wing of Captain Hughes, president of the Sydney Aero Club. It was here that I met Sir Keith Smith who, with his brother, had flown to Australia so many years before.

During the whole time I was in Sydney I do not think I had one spare moment. I was the guest of Admiral Sir Dudley de Chair, the Governor of New South Wales, at Government House, and every morning my day began with the entrance into my bedroom at 8.30 of Hughes, who presented the day's programme, invariably containing a succession of appointments and functions until well beyond midnight. I found myself making speeches night and day until our departure for Melbourne on Sunday morning.

It was a delightful trip over country very much like Wales or the Lowlands of Scotland, and though we had a little rain on the way we experienced no real difficulties.

According to plan a single machine met us about fifty miles out of Melbourne, while a little further on another escort picked us up, and thus we arrived over the aerodrome at Essendon.

Now there had been a record crowd of sixty-thousand people to greet us at Sydney, but at Melbourne we were amazed to find a crowd of at least a hundred and fifty thousand; in fact, one of the largest I have ever seen in my life. I looked at Ward through the window of the cabin; he looked back at me; and I think we were both a little overcome. It was obvious that the people of Australia were more alive than most – especially those at home – to the importance of aviation to the future of the Empire. I think it was for this reason that they turned out in such overwhelming numbers to greet the little bus which had brought us all the way from the home country.

As I looked down on the crowd beneath me I could see that it was ready to break through the barriers, and I realised that if I did not get down at once I should not be able to land at all because the ground

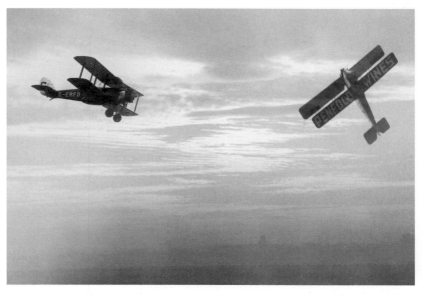

This enthusiastic welcome at Melbourne suggests a far from dry celebration awaits on the ground!

Cobham regarded his landing at Melbourne among the most perilous moments of the entire journey. The crowd, breaking through security cordons, posed a serious safety risk.

would soon be packed with humanity. A special clearing had been made in front of one of the hangars, to which I was supposed to taxi the machine, the plan being that railings would be erected round the aeroplane and all the addresses and such-like would be made from an adjacent platform. Before I landed I could see this would never work, and so as I neared the ground I decided to taxi as hard as I could up to the hangar immediately on landing, in the hope that the doors would be opened and I should be able to get inside the hangar before we were completely overrun.

The moment our wheels touched the ground the crowd on all sides broke the barriers and rushed at us. I turned the machine as quickly as I could and taxied full out for the hangar, while the crowd got denser and denser. They seemed to have an utter disregard for the propeller, which being an all-metal one would certainly have cut in half anyone it touched; behind, they were falling over and breaking our tail. At last the crowd became so overwhelming that we could not move, and I simply had to stop the propeller. Then there was a mighty rush, and the police and Air Force literally had to extract me from the cock-pit and carry me through that astounding throng towards the hangar. As they opened the hangar door to get me inside the crowd squeezed in too, whereupon I was rushed to the far corner and thrust into a small iron room where I was locked in. Thus it came about that within a few moments of landing at Melbourne I found myself a prisoner in a corrugated iron room with barred windows up to which boys were clambering, and a tin roof on which more boys were dancing!

A little later Colonel Brinsmead came in with the Lord Mayor and other representatives, and they told me the all the arrangements for my official reception had been dashed aside by the enthusiasm of the crowd. I feared for my machine, and was much relieved to hear

The 'thin blue line' attempts to hold back the crowd at Melbourne's Essendon Airport – not with great success.

Cobham's DH50 surrounded by sightseers in front of the hangars.

Opposite: Not a scene today's health and safety officials could feel happy about. People seem oblivious to the risk of serious injury from the fast-revving propeller. Cobham was besieged at Melbourne by a crowd that he estimated at over 150,000.

that it had been safely pushed into the hangar and that Ward was found to be still alive.

We spent a whole fortnight in Melbourne, during which time I think I worked about eighteen hours a day. Letters poured in from every part of Australia, and I felt it my duty to answer them in gratitude for their writers' kindness in taking such an interest in the enterprise. I was provided with a staff of secretaries and thus I was able to cope with the two thousand odd letters that I received.

I came to the conclusion that Australia was the most perfect country in the world for flying, and that aviation might very easily alter the whole national life of this great continent by means of the light aeroplane and the privately-owned aeroplane. The isolation problem on the out-back farms could be abolished entirely if every station had its own aircraft, because whereas at present it very often takes days to visit a friend or to get supplies, air-transport would reduce this to minutes or hours. I think I have said before that the continent

Pictured here with Melbourne's Lord Mayor and city officials, Cobham and Ward manage to keep smiling – just!

Although the Melbourne theatre is festively decked out in Cobham's honour, the audience seems strangely subdued.

is one vast natural aerodrome, and the climatic conditions – they never have fogs or blizzards or snow – permit 365 days' flying in the year.

Australia is alive to flying, and during my visit I noticed that three light aeroplane clubs came into being; one at Sydney, another at Melbourne, and a third at Adelaide. They were all using the little de Havilland Moth which had been developed at home, and in one of which in my earlier days I had managed to fly from London to Switzerland and back in a day.

During our stay at Melbourne we shifted our machine over to the Australian Air Force aerodrome at Point Cook, where every facility was given us to overhaul her. Ward set to work on the machine, assisted by Mr Capel of the Armstrong Siddeley Company, who had come out to Australia on business.

This interesting study shows Cobham and Ward at a Melbourne revue theatre (top left-hand box). In what was probably a hot, desultory atmosphere, several in the audience appear, like the two air heroes, to be less than overwhelmed by the performance.

Though called upon to be 'centre-stage', Cobham (centre, middle row) again appears to be numb with fatigue. Note the RAF 'wings' sported by the ladies of the revue.

On the return journey I hoped to put up a bit of a speed record, which would mean two big jumps a day. Now I knew this would be too much work for Ward because it entailed flying from dawn until sunset every day with but one brief halt at midday in which to refuel, thus leaving insufficient time for one man to attend to machine and engine in the available daylight. Therefore I asked Capel if he would care to fly back with us, for although the machine was already over-loaded as a seaplane I thought that by throwing some extra clothing overboard and lightening up all round we might be able to take his extra weight.

When the day came for our departure from Melbourne we said farewell to the many new-found friends who had done all in their power for us, and with many regrets flew on to Adelaide.

Time was getting short, for we had to get back to Darwin (to avail ourselves of the *Geranium*'s great assistance in putting on our floats again, before she sailed on her southern trip); so to our sorrow we were only able to stay one night in the delightful city of Adelaide.

The return flight was to be right up through the centre of the continent, more or less along the great telegraph route that runs from Adelaide due north to Darwin. Our first jump from Adelaide was to Oodnadatta, the terminus of the South Australian Railway. Our way took us up the eastern shores of the Gulf of St. Vincent, thence over vast tracks of arable land which I learnt afterwards is some of the finest corn land in the world. For miles and miles we flew over prosperous looking farms until we came to Spencer's Gulf along whose shores we cruised to Port Augusta. On again up the shores of Lake Torrens until we converged with the railway, and so we carried on passed Lake Eyre. We were now experiencing a very severe head wind and I doubted if we would be able to reach Oodnadatta on our petrol capacity. So we landed at a place called Marree where I knew we could get sufficient petrol to carry us on to Oodnadatta.

In this part of Australia it is possible to land practically anywhere, so when we came to Marree I simply put the machine down on the most convenient looking spot near the town. Very quickly everybody in that little outpost flocked over in their cars to greet us. We stayed long enough to re-fuel and then pushed on again for Oodnadatta, where we arrived in good time before sunset. We had left the rainy and cloudy weather far behind and were now in a land of permanent sunshine and blue skies, with hard rocky mountains on the horizon and vast open spaces below. The country reminded me very much of certain parts of Spain.

After a pleasant evening at Oodnadatta came the jump due north to Alice Springs. Soon after getting into the air I noticed that the character of the country was changing to one of bush and pasture, perhaps one of the greatest cattle countries in the world.

The only means I had of finding my way was by following the track of the telegraph line, which is distinguishable by the passage that has been cut through the bush, along the centre of which the telegraph posts run. Very often it was quite impossible to see any sign of the track immediately beneath me, and it was only by climbing to a great altitude and looking a long way ahead that I could pick up the definite straight line where it cut through odd stretches of bush before it became invisible again on the open plain.

Eventually we sighted the Macdonnell Range, said to be the oldest mountains in the world, and, just a few miles beyond, Alice Springs in the very centre of Australia. A landing ground had been prepared by Sergeant Stott who has so cleverly administered this area for the last ten or fifteen years and is generally looked upon as the great man of the district. Alice Springs is a beautiful place with a delightful climate and charming scenery, and a visibility so clear that my impression was that I could not take off from the aerodrome without running into the mountains. The Macdonnell Range towers up like a great rock wall overhanging Alice Springs and I was amazed to hear that it was at least three miles away. Owing to the wonderful visibility I had lost all conception of distance.

From Alice Springs we continued northward until we came to Newcastle Waters once more, but on the way we landed at a farm called Banka-Banka. It happened in this way. Before leaving Adelaide I had received an urgent telegram from a motor transport owner to carry a spare part up to Banka Banka where he had a car which had broken down. In the ordinary course he would have been delayed six or nine months until the spare arrived by the usual means of transport through central Australia, that is by camel. I understand that without the camel the interior of Australia certainly would never have been conquered. Now it is possible to make an aerodrome outside the front door of most farms or stations in Australia, and therefore when we arrived at Banka-Banka we just came down on the ground prepared for us and delivered the spare part, thus reducing the car owner's delay from six or nine months to exactly one week. Surely this is one good proof of the usefulness of aviation in Australia.

At Newcastle Waters our old silent friends were waiting to receive us and quickly helped to refuel our machine. As a little souvenir we had brought them a nice large ham; their yearly provision train which was coming up from the south by camel was already six months overdue, so our lump of bacon was much appreciated.

Then we took off again for Katherine, experiencing great heat on this part of the journey. I afterwards learnt that Daly Waters, which is half way between Katherine and Newcastle is one of the hottest places in Australia and often registers 105 and 110 in the shade.

We spent the night at Katherine under conditions somewhat similar to those at Newcastle Waters, and we wondered why, because there is no earthly reason why everything should not be made quite comfortable and pleasant at hardly any extra cost. We put up at the local hotel, a rambling shanty built mainly of batons and sheets of corrugated iron. Our host, an Irishman, was well content with his lot, having a family of five or six charming daughters who, he boasted did all the work and ran the place.

The following morning our host ran us out to the flying ground, about five minutes away, in his Ford; he had brought us in the night before and had also superintended the carrying of the petrol to the drome. Nevertheless I was surprised to receive a hotel bill of £3.10.0 for our meal and shakedown, and still more surprised when I paid it to hear our host muttering something about charging up his expenses to the Government. I quietly explained that the flight was run entirely on private contributions and that the Government had nothing at all to do with my expenses, which had to be paid out of the funds that I had collected. This was obviously a great surprise for our friend, who said 'What, Government not paying for this job?' and tried to give me back £2, but without success.

In the air once again we headed for Darwin, arriving according to plan on 2 September to find that HMS *Geranium* had returned from a cruise with the Governor-General to Broome and was already awaiting us in harbour. Furthermore they had despatched a party of men to the beach against our arrival. The tide was fairly low and I had no difficulty in landing on the sands. Half an hour later the scaffolding was up above our machine and she was being lifted from the ground so that the undercarriage could be unfastened. In the meantime the

Now re-equipped with floats, Cobham prepares to leave Darwin.

A final farewell to Australia, as Cobham sets out on the homeward flight.

floats were lifted off the jetty, lowered into the water and towed round to our beach, and the work of converting our aeroplane once more into a seaplane was quickly accomplished.

Commander Bennett of HMS *Geranium* begged me not to worry about the coming sea journey to Timor for, having ascertained the course we should take, he declared his intention of standing by at Darwin until news of our safe arrival at Kupang should reach him by wireless. In the event of that message failing to reach him within eight or nine hours, he would put to sea and follow up the bearing which I had taken and come in search of us. He asked me, in the event of our being unfortunate enough to have to land on the water, not to attempt to sail the seaplane by rigging up sheets and such-like, but just to wait quietly in our course because he would be able to allow in his reckoning for any drifting currents and thus stand a much better chance of finding us than if we sailed off our course in an endeavour to reach land on our own account.

On the morning of our departure we wheeled our seaplane down the beach on two wheels separated by a shaft through a hole in the floats. But when we had floated her on the water we found that the iron shaft that had been passed through the axle housing in the floats had jammed and we could not get it out. The only thing to be done was to saw through this iron bar, which was two inches in diameter. This took a long time and in the middle of the operation the saw was dropped in the sea and we had to get another one; so that our departure from Darwin was delayed so much that we knew we could not reach our original destination, namely Bima, before nightfall. We therefore had to content ourselves with making Kupang only that day.

CHAPTER V

THE FLIGHT HOME

It had been my ambition to lessen the distance in time between England and Australia by making a dash flight from Darwin. My plan was to make two jumps per day, keeping up anything from seven hundred to a thousand miles continually between dawn and sunset.

Our flight from Darwin to Kupang was just as successful as the outward journey had been and, owing to the fact that we had a following wind, it took about one and a half hours less time. On the following day we had another good flight from Kupang to Bima, and from Bima on again to Surabaya, doing over eight hundred miles. The day after we jumped from Surabaya to Batavia and from Batavia to Muntok. I remember arriving over Muntok and being undecided whether to carry on to Singapore without landing or not. I had sufficient petrol on board but I feared the daylight might fail, added to which it had begun to drizzle with rain, so decided to put down at Muntok for the night. It so happened that this decision altered the story of the whole flight, for had I carried on to Singapore that night and in consequence been ready to start the following morning for Penang and make Victoria Point the same night, I should have missed the worst monsoon storm of the whole season in Burma and might have been in England fifteen or sixteen days after leaving Darwin; but through losing that half-day we collided with a terrible storm which delayed us for days and days.

After spending the night at Muntok we departed early the next morning and arrived at Singapore about 9 a.m. After refuelling we lunched with the Colonial Secretary and then continued our journey under ideal conditions to Penang.

When we took off from Penang we were confident we were going
to be in Singapore, about eleven hundred miles away, that night. All
went well until, as we flew north, we lost the protection from the
monsoon afforded by the island of Sumatra. The moment we were
beyond its most northerly point we discovered that we were now in
the full blast of the monsoon sweeping across the Indian Ocean. The
weather entirely changed and in the space of a few miles we had run
into very heavy rain. The wondrous rock islands that we had seen on
the outward journey basking in brilliant sunshine, their vivid shades
of green contrasting with the bright blue of the sea, were now turned
to dark grey masses that loomed dimly through the mist and rain out
of the black water. Around me in every direction violent rain-storms
were falling, and as I flew north the storms which were blowing more
or less from the west drifted across my path. It was always a question as
to whether I should fly in front of the storm and get round that way
or whether I should fly round the back of the storm. For fifty or sixty
miles I was successful in dodging between these deluges without being
caught out, but at last I was completely surrounded and found myself
forced to go straight ahead through the downpour. The visibility now,
instead of being as on the outward journey sixty or seventy miles, was
reduced to a matter of yards, and this, coupled with the handicap of
indifferent maps, made finding my way most difficult. At last we were
completely buried in a heavy storm with no visibility at all, when
suddenly I sensed more than saw a particularly black mass in front of
me. I did a steep vertical bank just in time to avoid a gaunt rock island
rising five hundred feet out of the water. After this I turned and flew
back on my tracks into a brighter atmosphere, endeavouring to make
up my mind what to do for the best, and deciding that it was not safe
to go blindly on through such bad weather. In the cabin I think they
were beginning to realise that something was wrong. I believe Ward
had just wakened from a refreshing sleep, for usually, so Capel told me,
he slumbered blissfully through most of our troubles in the air.

After a little time I about turned and again attempted to fly between the storms ahead. We were now about thirty miles from the coast of Siam, south of the island of Puket. As we crept on, keeping low over the water, we could see the dark mountains of rock, sinister and forbidding through the haze of the rain-sodden atmosphere. At last I decided that it was impossible to carry on and that I must take shelter somewhere until such time as the weather cleared a little and gave me better visibility. About this time we were passing over an irregular island where I noticed on the leeward side the water was calm. There was also a little sandy beach near by and so I decided to land forthwith and attempt to lie at anchor until the weather improved.

We landed safely, and within a few seconds Ward and Capel were out on the floats. As I looked over the side I could see that right up to the supposed sandy beach the ocean bed was a mass of rocks, and what sand there was formed only a tiny fringe along the shore. It meant running the risk of knocking our floats in if by chance we should touch one of these rocks in the shallows. I therefore quickly decided to turn the craft about and head for the sea a little with the object of taxying down the coast in search of a better spot.

Taxying crossways over rollers was no easy matter, but luckily within a few hundred yards we found another little sheltered bay with a really good sandy beach. We decided to throw our anchor overboard and as I was reluctant to stop the engine before we were finally moored up, there was rather a big drag. When the final pull came Ward found to his dismay that he had not fastened the end of the rope to the hook on the floats so that it was too much for him and he was faced with either going overboard or leaving go. Thus it came about that we lost our anchor. The only thing to do now was to beach the bus, so I turned her head into the shore and as we gently drifted up the sands Ward and Capel jumped into the water and drew the floats up on to the silver-sand beach. The jungle on this island was dense and came right down to the water's edge, and we could see it would be impossible to penetrate it. Our first job was to lash our towing rope to the nearest palm tree, which held our machine in position. Ward and Capel then began to look around and decided they must begin by lighting a fire. It is true they were both in soaking wet bathing costumes, and though we were in the tropics the complete absence of sun made them feel cold; but I think too that the romance of the situation, coupled with memories of the reading of their early youth, were largely responsible for the lighting of the fire.

For my part I could see no romance about the situation at all. Here we were on an uninhabited island about forty miles from the mainland, right off the beaten track, with no prospects of food of any description other than our emergency rations, which I calculated would last about three days. We were simply locked in on this tiny beach with a dense wall of jungle behind us and giant rocks running out to sea on either side. Our only hope was that the rain would stop and we could get away from the place. However, Ward and Capel were ideal companions in these circumstances and made light of the whole adventure. The fire was quickly lit with the aid of petrol and a sheet was rigged up among the trees under which we stood for shelter from the downpour. Presently we realised that the tide was coming in, and where we were to get to when it reached the jungle we did not know. We were also anxious about our floats which were being constantly bumped on the beach as the tide lifted the craft, and we found it necessary to draw her up higher and higher every few minutes.

At last I decided that as the visibility was lengthening a fraction we must risk taking off, and so after striking our little camp and stamping out our famous fire, we turned our machine round in the water and headed on to the open sea.

We were on the leeward of the island, that is to say, as the wind was blowing strongly from the west we were under the eastern cliff in the region of down-currents – in fact in the very worst possible position for taking off. We could not get away due east into the open sea as this meant directly downwind and I knew that owing to the rollers we should never come unstuck. So I had to take off due north across what wind there was, at the same time riding the long-way of the rollers. It was a terrible business; we bumped and crashed along over the water, sometimes gathering up speed which lifted us high on to the step so that we were almost taking off; only to meet a severe breaker that would hit our floats with a terrific thud and cause me to shut off and lose what speed I had gained for fear the thing would happen again. I made two such attempts to get off and failed; but the third time I hung on to it and at last I felt the machine stagger into the atmosphere. Once we bounced off the water I knew I only had to keep the machine in the air for a couple of seconds for her to gain sufficient air-speed to climb away, and finally we found ourselves cruising along in the down-currents of this dreary lee shore, whose aspect could be so utterly different in the sunshine.

I soon picked up my bearings and was successful in steering safely through several heavy showers until we came to the north-east corner of the island of Puket. Here we turned up a narrow creek which separated the island from the mainland. Once through this creek I knew we were on the main coastline which would bring us up direct to Victoria Point, about a hundred and thirty miles further on.

Unfortunately the rain had been too much for our propeller, which was of wood, and when I heard a whistling noise ahead and felt a very bad vibration I knew that the fabric was coming off, so I finally decided to land at Tanoon.

We alighted easily on the water and quietly beached the machine on the soft golden sand in front of the village. As soon as we had tied up and made her secure we were surrounded by a party of happy Siamese, of whose language we understood no more than they did of ours. We were right opposite the police hut and they very efficiently took charge of affairs for us. I discovered they had quite a good road from the village up inland, and so I decided to get to the nearest telegraph office and send messages to Victoria Point and Penang as to our whereabouts.

Before leaving, I noticed that one of our undercarriage struts was bent and surmised that we had done this in taking off from the lonely island. I left Ward and Capel to do their best to repair the damage, which happened to be on the opposite side of the same strut that had given out in the Bandar Abbas episode, and then, jumping into a motor car that these kind folks had procured, I set off in search of a telegraph office.

After journeying from one place to another I found that though there were many telegraph offices none of them was in working order, and it took me about three hours and much travelling to find a post office that could take our message.

The country here is very beautiful and when the sun began to shine I was full of hope of getting off that day for Victoria Point. Therefore I dashed back in the car to Tanoon, only to suffer the rude shock of finding our seaplane high and dry out of the water with the tide out at least a couple of hundred yards. I was rather annoyed with my little crew for allowing this to happen, especially as the sun was shining and the weather conditions were ideal for taking off on our next jump but they explained that in order to repair the broken strut they had to lift the tail high in the air. I happened to be looking round our floats at this juncture, the rear portions of which, owing to the shelving of the beach, were in the, air, when I noticed that water was trickling out of a hole in one of the floats on to the sand. In other words, the float was punctured and full of water, which was now trickling out owing to its different position. This of course meant another repair job, and so while Capel dug a hole in the sand beneath the float so that he could work from below, Ward undid the inspection plates at the top and found the hole that had doubtless been made during our adventure on the lonely island.

However, we had on board spare pieces of metal to make such a repair, and by a process of nuts and bolts and some white lead that we happened to find in the village, an excellent patch was made. By dint of sheer hard work and the light of a lamp, Ward and Capel had our machine air-worthy again about an hour after sunset.

That night we slept in the police hut, where they served us a wonderful meal of soup, stewed chicken and potatoes. Tinned biscuits were available and bottles of soda water were found, and I for one was happy in the thought that we were not still on our uninhabited island.

By ten o'clock the tide had risen sufficiently for us to refloat the seaplane, and so by the light of lamps and with the assistance of two rowing boats we towed her out into the inky blackness of the night, and anchored her safely at a convenient distance from the shore. We were preparing to row back to the shore when suddenly a launch appeared on the scene. It transpired that the Governor of Puket, who, was also a Prince of the Royal House of Siam, had heard of our predicament and had sent his secretary over at that late hour to render any assistance we might require. He had also sent a huge hamper of provisions so that our commissariat should not fail, and in view of our nationality our royal patron had tactfully included a bottle of whisky and some soda-water. We were much touched by this gracious attention and deeply grateful for such unmerited courtesy.

It rained most of the night and all the next morning, and I was beginning to think we should be there for days, when late in the afternoon there was a lull. It happened that there was a mining engineer from the north who was passing through Tanoon at this time on his way over the ferry for Puket, and he advised us to push on to Victoria Point at once. Of course we lost no time in acting on this advice and were soon in the air, racing for Victoria Point. We got there in about an hour and a half, passing through just one or two slight showers and an atmosphere that was generally heavy and overcast.

At Victoria Point, although they were not expecting us, they soon had us in tow and tied up to a mooring. That night we went to bed full of hopes of reaching Rangoon on the following day, and wakened in the morning to clearer weather which was only slightly marred by a dark and heavy horizon away to the south-west whence all the bad weather was coming.

However, we did not allow this to depress us, and the dawn found us down at our machine. Soon after six o'clock we were in the air, heading north-west up the coastline. The further north we went the worse the weather became, and after defying several banks of rain we were finally defeated by a deluge through which it was impossible to fly. Apart from the fact that the visibility was rendered almost nil, the force of the rain literally blinded me. It obliterated all vision through my goggles so that they had to be removed, and I was forced to take shelter behind the screen in such a way that I could just look out sideways with out getting the full blast of water in my face.

We were obliged to about-turn, when to my dismay I found that all the bad weather we had seen on the horizon at the start had raced up behind us. There was nothing for it but to fight our way back to Victoria Point, and all along that rocky coastline we were dodging between the centres of the densest rain-storms I have ever experienced. Sometimes it was necessary to circle round and round in a well of moderately clear atmosphere until the heaviest banks of falling water had spent themselves and we could dodge through again. In this manner we made slow progress southward, with the constant dread of being caught out and forced to land on the water until after about an hour and a half of this terrible flying, Victoria Point came once more into view and we managed to get down on the water again.

We went straight to the rest house bungalow, which was put at our disposal, and there we changed into dry clothes kindly lent by the District Officer and the doctor, for at Victoria Point there is a hospital.

In spite of this experience I would not say that it is going to be impossible to fly through the monsoon, for if we had had wireless weather reports we should never have attempted our flight that morning. A regular air-route would of course have a proper wireless organisation all along the line with frequent weather reports so that the service could be maintained all through the monsoon period, although perhaps not such a regular one as in the fine weather season.

The following day was again bad, although it cleared in the evening a bit; but after my experience of the day before I was not out to start again until a more or less permanent change in the weather took place. The wireless station was not working and we therefore had no communication with the outer world at Victoria Point; but by sailing over to the mainland of Siam at Ranawng where there is a telegraph station it is possible to get messages through. On Sunday the rainfall was five inches, and with no available weather reports I was timid about going ahead.

Luckily I had managed to get a telegram off to England saying we were at Victoria Point on the Friday after our bad experience, for the message that we tried to get through on Saturday were returned on Monday because the telegraph line had broken down in Siam. So we were now stranded at Victoria Point with no communication whatever with the rest of the world.

We were there for four days during which time it rained anything up to five inches each day. Of course the whole idea of our dash back to England was entirely spoilt, but I consoled myself with the fact that we were making a really practical survey of monsoon conditions in Burma, and that with this experience the value of our report would be far greater than had we missed this severe period altogether.

We were not idle during those four days at Victoria Point. I worked hard on arrears of correspondence and reports of machine and aircraft and the trip in general which would otherwise have been left until my return home. Ward and Capel worked hard polishing up the propellers, cleaning out the machine, overhauling the engine and reorganising our kit, and every day seemed to be fully occupied.

It rained and rained night and day, so that the poor old bus was wet through and through. At last we found it necessary to bore holes in the cabin floor in order to let the water run out.

When Tuesday arrived there seemed to be a definite clearing in the atmosphere. The barometer was rising steadily and on the advice of the doctor, who kept the weather reports, we pushed on again.

We had a good run for nearly two hundred miles until we came to Mergui. The atmosphere was fairly clear although the day was dull, and we flew low so that we could be observed. I learnt later that the moment we passed over Mergui the whole world was informed of our whereabouts, for they instantly flashed a message through to Rangoon and from there it was distributed. I do not think we had realised the anxiety we had caused through being isolated at Victoria Point.

After Mergui we ran into bad weather again but the rain was not quite heavy enough to stop us from going forward, and so we flew through four hundred miles of rain right up the Burma coast to Moulmein and across the bay to Rangoon.

The next day it was raining heavily and knowing the difficulty of flying between Rangoon and Akyab I thought it wise to have a special weather report before continuing the journey. I therefore sent an urgent telegram to Simla, which was fourteen hundred miles away, and an hour and a quarter later I had a long and detailed reply, which was a record in telegraph service speed. They almost forbade my departure from Rangoon in view of the bad prospects, and sure enough an hour later there was such a heavy deluge that the machine had to be hauled up to the hangar so that she could be kept dry.

The hauling up of the machine at Rangoon on the return trip was almost as comic as on the outward journey. I conclude that the coolies have a great objection to getting wet, for these gentlemen, clad only in a loin-cloth, always carry an umbrella. Just as a gang of them had been placed in line ready to pull the machine up, the rain came down heavily, and as we turned to give the order to haul we found to our amazement that each man had raised an umbrella to protect his precious body. I shall never forget Ward's utter bewilderment at this sight. Here were labourers with umbrellas up, and as he said, not a blessed stitch on their bodies. He rushed along the line, seizing the umbrellas and flinging them aside, while the coolies stood stupifed. Anyway the episode provided a diversion for the Europeans who had gathered round, for they were in convulsions of laughter.

On the following day we were able to leave Rangoon, and after successfully zig-zagging between sunshine and storm we arrived at

Calcutta in sunshine. We were ready to go the next morning but again the weather report from Simla was unfavourable. It appeared that the same old storm with which we had collided sixteen hundred miles further south, north of Penang, and which we had been unable to get ahead of right up the coast of Burma, was now raging at Allahabad, six hundred miles north of us, which happened to be our destination after Calcutta.

So we waited another day at Calcutta and then we were informed by the port authorities that we must go the next day because a bore was coming up the river. A bore is a great tidal wave which occurs at certain seasons of the year, and is a solid bank of water about four feet high which floods up the river as the tide comes in. The authorities feared the effect of this upon our seaplane, because owing to the fact that the surface of the river is raised about four feet in as many seconds, it had been known to wreck a number of craft on the Hooghli on previous occasions.

Luckily the day was fairly fine and we were able to continue our journey to Allahabad without much trouble. We stayed the night and then, with the weather report to the effect that we might meet a few local showers, we continued to Delhi the following day.

As we were passing over Cawnpore we ran into one of the so-called local showers, which meant flying through a rain storm ten miles thick during which I feared more than once that I should be compelled to land on the river. However, we struggled through to Delhi where we found they had shifted our mooring spot. When we had got safely hitched up ready to refuel, the rope broke and we found ourselves drifting downstream at about six or seven knots. Luckily we were in mid-stream and the banks on either side were sand or mud, but it was an awkward situation, especially as I knew there was a weir lower down the river. I quickly decided that the best thing to do was to make the machine drift over on to the sandy bank on the far side of the river, and with a small paddle that we had aboard Ward worked heroically until it broke. This was unfortunate because we were now within twenty feet of a convenient sand-bank.

I was doing my best with the mooring pole, but we were on the point of missing our goal when Capel jumped into the water and, catching hold of the connecting bar between the floats, started to swim hard and push the machine ashore. Ward followed suit and thus by swimming hard and pushing we made the machine drift gently on to the soft mud bank where we beached her without any harm. Capel then ran ashore with the anchor which he buried deep in the soft mud, and so we were held securely in position.

The wind was in a convenient direction for our take off and we were soon on our way again to Bahawalpur. Here again we found our mooring had been shifted but luckily a launch was available which took us in tow.

The next day we had another successful flight down the Indus to where we were able to put in a fair amount of time on both machine and engine, and as it was early in the day I had a moment in which to get off my dispatches and make preparations for our progress down the Gulf.

We were now picking up speed, doing five to six hundred miles a day, so that we hoped to be home within the next five or six days. But at Chahbar on the following morning we found that although we were successful in alighting on the water, we could not get off again on account of the unsuitable direction of the wind and the permanent rollers. Mr Tomlinson, who was in charge of the telegraph station at Chahbar, told us we had better wait until the next morning when the sea would be calmer and the rollers would be less. Unfortunately the following morning there was a total lack of wind with very little abatement of the rollers, so that we were still unable to rise. We had about three attempts and I was almost giving up in despair, when suddenly a gentle breeze sprang up from the east. I decided to take off along the lee shore of the Cape, which was protected a bit from the rollers but which meant my taking off eventually over the land.

After another attempt had failed and I was on the point of giving up the attempt, we came unstuck and a few seconds later we were over the beach and gradually climbing.

About midday we were flying over Laft, and landed to find that the British Consul at Bandar Abbas had sent the famous 'Felix Jones' to put down moorings for us, and in perfectly calm and sheltered waters, such as I had expected would prevail from its position on the map, we moored our craft.

A Persian clerk from the Consulate and several native servants had been awaiting us for days. They had erected a tent and had improvised a field kitchen. The camp was situated on a high spot amid charming mountain scenery on the island of Quisham, about half a mile from the dilapidated Persian village. Thus we very soon found ourselves in the cool tent through which gentle breezes played, enjoying a delightful lunch, followed by a little sleep. Then much refreshed we got to the necessary work on machine and engine, and as the sun went down and our work was finished, the servants brought the table out of the tent and laid it for dinner. After dinner when we had finished our smokes, the camp beds were put round the table and we turned in under the ceiling of a star-lit sky.

We were getting nearer home now, and as I lay on my back and looked up at the milky way I estimated how many days it would be before we reached London. I felt the worst was over. Although we had seemed a long way on our outward journey when we were at Bandar Abbas, now on the return trip, having covered over twenty thousand miles, we seemed almost home.

Soon after sunrise, when we had breakfasted, we said goodbye to our kind hosts and were soon in the air heading on our way to Bushire. Here we found friends awaiting us in a launch with ample refreshments, and after a quick fill-up of our machine we took the air for Baghdad.

All along the Gulf I had been greatly troubled by the heat. Day by day it got hotter and hotter, and our poor old Jaguar engine which had now done so many miles without a complete overhaul, was having a very hard time, especially in getting the machine off the water in this boiling atmosphere.

It was on the flight from Bushire to Baghdad that I think we experienced almost the greatest heat of the whole trip, especially at the point of passing the extreme head of the Persian Gulf. It got so hot that the oil coming out of the engine was 76 Centigrade, and I estimated that the atmosphere at ground level must have been about 115 in the shade.

I found it most difficult to climb because this naturally needed more throttle, which again caused greater heat, and so having reached about two thousand five hundred feet with a steadily rising temperature, I throttled down and continued at this altitude. I do not think I should have worried if I had been on the outward journey with my engine fresh, but it was my ambition to complete the Sir Charles Wakefield Flight of Survey with the same machine and the same engine with which we started, and thus create a world record for the longest distance flight with the same engine.

It was getting late in the afternoon when I decided to land at Basra instead of making Baghdad that day, principally because Ward wanted to see some of his old companions. We landed safely and were soon among old friends. Next morning we were again flying northward for Baghdad with the object of refuelling and getting to Alexandretta without delay.

With a fully-loaded machine (which really meant a big over-load) we managed to get off the water at Baghdad in the hot midday sun and then climbed away towards the River Euphrates. The heat was terrific and our temperature again rose quickly but, by nursing the engine and assisted by a kindly up-current which seemed to come from nowhere, we got to about three thousand feet.

Thus we progressed, passing over Ana, then Deir-ez-Zor, on to Rakka, until we came to the spot where the Euphrates bends abruptly north. At this point we crossed over the land, leaving Aleppo to the south, and after skimming the mountains once more, found ourselves suddenly with the Mediterranean before us and Alexandretta below, nestling on the shores of a delightful bay.

Our good friend, Mr Catoni, the British Consul, was awaiting us with his launch and quickly had us in the harbour. While Capel inspected the engine, Ward refuelled and attended to the machine, so that before sunset we were in Mr Catoni's motor car speeding out of Alexandretta to his charming villa two thousand feet up in the hills behind the town. It was one of the most perilous motor rides I have ever had. I was far more 'windy' than I had ever been during a flight, for we did a succession of about fifty hairpin bends, skirting over hanging cliffs at a speed ranging from fifteen to fifty miles an hour.

The next trip took us along the coast of Turkey to Leros, where the Italian Commander was waiting to receive us with congratulations on our flight.

Ample supplies of fuel were available, for from Karachi to London the British Petroleum Company had laid down stocks of B.P. spirit, and after a quick refuel we reluctantly took off from this beautiful harbour and headed out over the Ægean Sea towards Athens.

Here again we were among old friends and, after spending a night with Major Buck of the Blackburn Company, we again took off for our next destination, which was Naples.

When Corfu had faded from view behind us we ran into a misty atmosphere and low cloud, which made our trip seem longer than it actually was; but at last we reached the Gulf of Taranto and then crossed the mountains of Calabria to the sea on the far side. Here we experienced great difficulty, and after climbing to about seven thousand feet in order to clear not only the mountains themselves but also the heavy cloud banks that were forming in all directions as well, we managed to dodge through and get underneath the clouds on the western coast of Italy.

Here the weather had completely changed and the western horizon was a mass of heavy black cloud and thunder storms. The visibility shortened and very soon we ran into rain. As we passed between the mainland and Capri it struck me how unlike the popular imagination of such a place it looked.

Soon we were landing by Nisida Island in the Bay of Naples; we quickly filled up, but owing to the bad weather it did not seem possible that we should be able to reach Marseilles before dark, for we had already lost much time in our detour over the mountains of southern Italy.

However, the Commandant of Nisida advised us not to stay there, explaining that if the wind got much worse we should never get out of the harbour. He recommended the seaplane base of Orbetello further up the coast where there was an excellent enclosed water from which could get off under any conditions.

So we pushed on again through heavy rain, and a little later we reached Orbetello.

I had been very fortunate before starting this flight in arranging with three separate petrol companies to lay down supplies between London and Australia. All three of these concerns laid down their supplies from the purely patriotic motive of supporting British pioneer aviation work. It is certainly a long-sighted policy on their part, for it undoubtedly means much to the development of Empire trade.

The British Petroleum Company provided B.P. spirit from London to Charbar; The Burma Oil Company laid supplies from Karachi to Rangoon; and the Shell Mex Company put down stocks of their spirit from Victoria Point right through the Dutch East Indies to Melbourne, so that in this respect I had been thoroughly well looked after.

The flight from Orbetello to Marseilles was full of interest for as we pushed out over the sea from the Italian coast we could see on our right the island of Elba and away to our left the great rock island of Monte Cristo; while a little later we crossed the northern coast of Corsica, out over the Mediterranean to the Riviera coast line.

The gale blowing from the north had held us back considerably, so I knew there was no time to be lost when we got to the seaplane base at Marignane, if we were to fill up and be off again to reach Paris before nightfall. We found the B.P. agent awaiting us with a very elaborate pumping apparatus, so that we refuelled without delay and were ready to start on the next stage of our journey up the Rhone Valley to Paris.

I was keen to give the machine a bit of a wash down because I did not want to arrive in London smothered in Castrol oil. This excellent lubricant, though undoubtedly the finest in the world on which to run an engine to the uttermost parts of the earth and back, is not a pleasing mixture with which to anoint one's clothes or those of honoured guests inspecting the seaplane. And so at every stop on the latter part of the return flight a little washing down was done.

I was trying hard to reach London by a certain date in accordance with arrangements made, and had already received long telegrams of congratulation and invitation to various functions from Sir Charles Wakefield and I knew if anything went wrong in this last stage of the journey it would mean disappointment not only to me, but to those at home.

The first part of the trip from Marseilles was right up the Rhone valley, where the gale was against us at forty miles an hour, and I thought we should never reach Paris on time. I was growing rather alarmed at the bumps we encountered as we flew up the narrow gorge, and eventually I decided to get out of the Rhone valley and fly over the mountains into the valley of the Loire, where I hoped the wind would not be so strong against us. We were heavily loaded and up to that time had received down-currents which necessitated our opening out considerably in order to climb. But suddenly I noticed we were automatically gaining height, which meant we had struck a great up-current, so by gently coaxing the nose upward and giving just a little more throttle, we took advantage of this up-current to climb to an altitude of five thousand feet in a very short time. We were soon over the mountains and following up the valley of the Loire, cruising passed St Etienne, Roanne and Nevers, flying low to avoid a head wind, until at last Fontainebleau came on the horizon.

I shall never forget the last part of that flight to Paris, because in order to avoid the wind which was against us we flew at an altitude of about a hundred feet over hill and dale and rocky crag in a seaplane, when engine-failure, although not tremendously dangerous would have meant perhaps the ruin of a very splendid flight. I mention this merely to show the confidence of my crew and myself in our engine, despite the fact that it had put up a world's record for a long distance flight across the world without a complete overhaul. Yet here, on the last lap of this great test, we were flying with impunity just as though we were starting out with a fresh engine.

The same applied to our de Havilland seaplane, which had been through every sudden climatic change it was possible to experience. Yet here was this old war-horse flying just as perfectly as it ever flew, with rigging intact, cruising at over a hundred miles an hour at the end of its third great Empire flight.

When we reached Paris we circled the south-west suburbs and came up the Seine to Sartrouville, where we landed on the river in calm water, effected by the closed lock-gates. A telegram awaited me from Sir Samuel Hoare, Secretary of State for Air, requesting me to arrive the following day at Westminster, landing on the Thames in front of the Houses of Parliament by 2.5 p.m.

Hats off to the returning heroes, as Cobham makes his first approach over the Thames.

Thus it came about that on 1 October 1926, we took off from the Seine at Paris and did our last little hop over France to the Channel, then on over Hastings and Maidstone to Rochester. It was here that we realised, perhaps for the first time, how much the British public were interested in our flight. The banks of the Medway were lined with people and I know that we were all three astonished. But the best moment of all was when flying low over Short Brothers Aircraft Works on the banks of the river we saw that every hand had turned out to welcome us back to the place we had started from – and with the same pair of metal floats on our seaplane that they had built for us three months before.

We felt we should like to land, but they were waiting for us at Westminster, so after circling two or three times we pushed on up the Thames towards London.

Cobham flies down wind over Westminster Bridge before reversing course to land on the Thames.

Standing room only for the estimated million people who crowded onto the Embankment and Westminster Bridge for Cobham's arrival. Note the adventurous souls on the GLC building's chimney stacks.

Cobham's 26,000-mile round trip was a breathtaking achievement to a 1920s population still attuned to horse and cart transport.

2.26 p.m. on 1 October 1926 and the final touch–down on the Thames.

One million people were estimated to welcome Cobham's arrival in front of the Houses of Parliament. Note the hardy souls perched on the GLC's chimney stacks.

Above: Capel and Ward make G-EBFO secure on the fast-flowing Thames. Note the density of the onlookers on the far embankment.

Opposite above: A man with a mission completed! His wife and the world's press await him.

Opposite below: Cobham leads his two engineers, Ward and Capel, up the steps into the media spotlight.

Even above the roar of our engine we could hear the steamers hooting a welcome as we passed over Victoria Docks and down to Tower Bridge. It was the luncheon hour, and I fear that many a clerk was late that afternoon in returning to his office, for all the bridges were massed with white faces looking upwards, and every warehouse had its windows full. As we passed over Blackfriars and Waterloo bridges I looked through to Ward and Capel; they were taking photographs.

All three of us were overwhelmed by such a great reception and I think in this triumphant moment all the trials and worries of our long flight seemed to have been well worth while.

After flying up the Thames as far as Hammersmith, in response to requests by telegram, we turned back and, circling Westminster once

Above: Worth waiting for! Gladys and Alan Cobham reunited after the three-month separation.

Opposite above: King Abdulla and Crown Prince Hirohito were among the mixed gathering listening to Cobham's 'glad to be home' speech.

Opposite below: Now the centre of international attention, Cobham converses with, left to right: Sir Samuel Hoare, Lord Wakefield, Sir Sefton Brancker (Director of Civil Aviation), and J.S. Whitely; Cobham's wife and parents are immediately alongside and behind Branker.

Above: Capel, Cobham and Ward pose for the camera on the steps leading up from the Thames to the House of Commons terrace.

Opposite above: Proud to be British! The Cobhams are accompanied by Sir Samuel Hoare (behind) and J.S. Whitely, Speaker of the House.

Opposite below: Submerged in an admiring crowd, the Cobhams are driven past another figure of national importance, Oliver Cromwell.

THE DAILY GRAPHIC, OCTOBER 2, 1926.

£5,000 IN SCHOLARSHIPS: FULL DETAILS ON MONDAY.

DAILY GRAPHIC

PUT YOUR
CLOCK BACK
TO-NIGHT.

No. 11,470.　　Registered as a Newspaper.　　SATURDAY, OCTOBER 2, 1926.　　ONE PENNY.

THE NATION WELCOMES COBHAM HOME.

Mr. Cobham on the Terrace reading the King's telegram congratulating him "heartily on the successful termination of yet another historical flight." It was handed him by Sir Samuel Hoare, the Air Minister (right). The Speaker is on the left.

Mrs. Alan Cobham greeting her husband when he landed at the Speaker's steps at the House of Commons yesterday on finishing his 28,000 miles flight to Australia and back. Smiling on the left is the Speaker, Mr. J. H. whitley, and Sir Charles Wakefield, organiser of the flight, is second from the right.

Mr. Cobham's aeroplane passing a few feet above Westminster Bridge, which was crowded, despite the police efforts to keep it clear. In the background is St. Thomas's Hospital. After going up to Hammersmith, Cobham returned and landed on the Thames, opposite the Houses of Parliament. Other pictures of the great welcome to him will be found in our middle pages.

Above: Cobham's joyous homecoming was well covered by the media, as typically depicted on the *Daily Graphic*'s front page.

Opposite above: Repeat performance! The DH50 is again the centre of attention at Selfridges' Oxford Street store. See also picture on page 67 after Cobham's return from his African adventure.

Opposite below: Young Geoffrey Cobham with a new-found friend following his father's return. Normal family life for both Geoffrey and younger brother Michael, born in 1927, proved difficult in the wake of Sir Alan's high public profile.

Sir Alan Cobham was a highly influential figure in Britain's aviation development. His devotion to making the country 'air-minded' was legendary and led, in the 1930s, to his enormously successful touring air displays and founding of Flight Refuelling Ltd, a company which ultimately proved to be the cornerstone of Cobham plc – today a £1 billion provider to the world's aerospace and defence industries.

more, I prepared to land on the water. It was low tide and the wind was blowing across the river, so that the air was blanketed by the Houses of Parliament. This made our landing rather difficult, so I circled twice to have a look at the proposition. I decided to side-slip in over Westminster Bridge and, having done this successfully, we made a fair landing on the water beyond St Thomas's Hospital.

Without delay we were taken in tow by a motor boat, and then, a little bewildered, we came ashore and were conducted up the Palace Landing Stairs, so rarely used in history, to the Terrace of the House.

I think it was the proudest moment of my life when I found my wife waiting at the top to greet me.

Then there were Mr Whitley, the Speaker, Sir Samuel Hoare, Secretary of State for Air, and Sir Sefton Brancker, Director of Civil Aviation, all waiting to receive us; and one who so ardently believes in aviation for the Empire, Sir Charles Wakefield; and again, my old chief, Captain de Havilland, who had designed the aircraft.

We were led to the Terrace where we were officially received by the Lord Chamberlain, and I do not know how Ward and Capel felt about it, but to me it was a very great moment.

At the close of that tremendous day I think I went to bed convinced that at last the public realised the importance of aviation to every Briton, and — what is more — I felt that its imagination was aroused in support of this good cause. I hope I was right.

POSTSCRIPT

COLIN CRUDDAS FRAeS

In 1920 two South African Air Force officers, Lieutenant-Colonel Pierre van Ryneveld and Flight Lieutenant Christopher Quintin Brand, became the first airmen to fly from England to the Cape. Their journey took forty-five days and because of crashes along the route, a total of three aircraft, two Vickers Vimys and one DH9 were required to complete the flight.

Little further official interest was shown until March 1925 when Sir Samuel Hoare, then Under Secretary of State for Air, announced that long-distance flights to South Africa and Nigeria were to be carried out by the Royal Air Force.

This intention coincided with that of Alan Cobham (later Sir Alan) who, following a successful first round-trip by air to India in 1924–25, had become enthused at the prospect of starting a commercial air-route to the Cape. Having gathered sufficient sponsorship, principally that of philanthropist Lord Wakefield, he set about organising what he grandly called the 'Empire League Imperial Airways Survey' – although at that stage, Imperial Airways was more concerned with consolidating its European air route structure and the future development of regular air services to the Middle and Far East.

Not mentioned by Cobham in his post-flight memoirs is the worry he felt that such a long separation, so soon after his four month visit to India, would put a severe strain on his marriage. In the event, his wife, Gladys, offered her total support and made it clear, as she would frequently do so throughout Cobham's many faceted career, that he was 'doing the right thing'!

His epic London–Cape–London round-trip was a first time venture that required detailed planning of the highest order. The provisioning of fuel, oil and spares in places few people had ever heard of, usually several hundred miles apart, involved complicated arrangements that often took weeks of correspondence to put in place. Somehow it all worked. But equally remarkable is the fact that whilst primarily absorbed with ensuring the success of the South African exercise, Cobham was also entertaining thoughts for a similar flight to and from Australia soon after his return.

His book, *My Flight To The Cape And Back*, is, even today, a highly readable account of trying to link the Empire by air, and illustrates the immense difficulties that faced the route-blazing pioneers. He demonstrated beyond doubt, the feasibility of future air travel in Africa, given the political and commercial will to provide the proper infrastructure, and that daily distances of some 700 miles were within the capabilities of currently available aircraft. All this he recorded in a final report to Imperial Airways. However, a cloud appeared on Cobham's horizon in the shape of Captain Tony Gladstone, a director of the Blackburn Aeroplane Co.'s subsidiary North Sea Aerial and General Transport Co. Although the firm's title would hardly suggest an interest in Africa, Gladstone, having been given the remit to develop business opportunities overseas, had already seen a vast potential for air travel in East and Central Africa.

It was, therefore, almost inevitable that Cobham and Gladstone, both highly ambitious and opportunistic individuals would find themselves either in serious competition or, more sensibly, able to combine their adventuresome talents to mutual advantage.

The manner in which this potentially troublesome situation was resolved is well recounted in Sir Alan Cobham's own story of his 1928 journey round Africa, *Twenty Thousand Miles In A Flying-Boat*, now republished by Tempus.

Cobham's triumphant return from South Africa, greatly rein-forced his reputation as Britain's premier airman. It also fuelled his need to produce another 'rabbit from the hat', even more impressive than the last, and what better than a route-proving flight to Australia? The only previous flights to this far distant continent had been the one-way homeward journey by ex-servicemen Captain Ross Smith and his crew, and Lieutenants Parer and McIntosh in 1919–20, when several other attempts proved unsuccessful. No one had then con-sidered a two-way trip. Cobham, however, though possessed of great confidence, found himself drained from the effort of pre-flight prep-arations before, just three months after his return from the Cape, he set off from Rochester for Australia.

Again, his adventures are well chronicled in his book 'Australia and Back', with his most poignant thoughts being his reflections on the loss of his flight engineer, Arthur Elliott, in such tragic circumstances.

In today's world of 'round-the-clock news' and celebrity over-expo-sure, it is difficult to imagine the intensity of public adulation afforded to air pioneers such as Cobham, 'Bert' Hinkler and Amy Johnson. It must be recognised however, that the overwhelming praise they received belonged in an era when it was rare indeed for most people to ever get a first-hand glimpse or see a moving image of notable public figures. Accordingly, the arrival of these pilots following their coura-geous epic flights to Australia was greeted by welcoming crowds that would equal those attending present day top-ranking rock star events.

Knighted after his return to England from Australia, Sir Alan Cobham went on to form, in the early 1930s, his touring National Aviation Day Display which provided some 1,000 air shows at loca-tions throughout Britain. His later career was mainly concerned with the development of techniques and equipment for air refuel-ling. Flight Refuelling Ltd, the company he founded for this purpose in 1934 was, though unforeseen at that time, to become the corner-stone of what is now Cobham plc, a worldwide organisation serving the aerospace and defence industries. Sir Alan Cobham, KBE, AFC, died on 21 October 1973, aged seventy-nine.

Also published by Tempus:

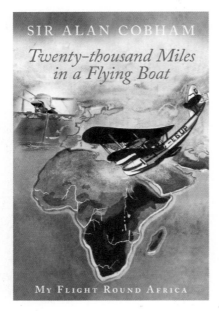

SIR ALAN COBHAM

Twenty-thousand Miles in a Flying Boat

MY FLIGHT ROUND AFRICA

Twenty-thousand Miles in a Flying Boat: My Flight Round Africa

Sir Alan Cobham

978-0-7524-4181-8

Sir Alan's flight round Africa in a Singapore seaplane that began in November 1927 laid the foundation of the Through-Africa Air Route. Starting at Rochester in Kent before crossing France and the Mediterranean, the route went via Malta, Egypt, East Africa through Kenya and Nyasaland, from Beira to Lagos, across to the Ivory Coast, from Freetown to Cape Bojador and through the Canaries, this historic journey essentially navigated the coast of Africa. Accompanying her husband throughout the six-month journey, Lady Cobham also established a record for air travel by a woman.

This is Sir Alan Cobham's first-hand account of his journey; first published in 1930, this edition is illustrated with over fifty photographs from the trip, including some previously unpublished and straight from the family archive

Sir Alan Cobham was Britain's premier pioneering aviator and a great figure in the history of aviation. Colin Cruddas is the Cobham family archivist. He has unearthed some new treasures for the revised edition; this is his fifth book for Tempus.

If you are interested in purchasing other books published by Tempus,
or in case you have difficulty finding any Tempus books in your local bookshop,
you can also place orders directly through our website
www.tempus-publishing.com